THE BOOK OF INDIAN-CRAFTS
AND COSTUMES

The Book of Indian-Crafts and Costumes

BERNARD S. MASON

Drawings By
Frederic H. Kock

THE RONALD PRESS COMPANY · NEW YORK

CONTENTS

Riders of the Plains and Roamers
  of the Woods   1
War-bonnet   2
Preparing the War-bonnet Feathers 3
Assembling the War-bonnet   4
The Major Plume   6
Setting the War-bonnet   7

Chippewa Feather Crest   8
Horn Headdress   10
Woodland Hat   11
Beaded Headbands   12
Forehead Rosettes   14
Rosette Designs   17
Turbans and Hair Feathers   18

Hair Roach	20	Dancing Bells	70
Top Feathers	24	Dance Rattles	72
Feather Roach	26	Turtle Rattles	73
Hair Bustles and Rosettes	28	Bullroarers and Moraches	74
Feather Bustles	30	War Clubs	75
Sioux Bustles	32	Making Rawhide	76
Bustle Tricks	34	Making Buckskin	78
Oklahoma Bustles	37	Drums	80
Butterflies	40	Drumsticks	83
U-Shaped Bustles with Spikes	41	Shields	84
Sunbursts	42	Coup-sticks and Shields	87
Crow	43	Dance Fans	88
Bustle Styles	44	Ornamental Feathers	89
Anklets	46	Parfleche of the Plains	90
Leg-Bands	47	Birchbark of the Woods	91
Moccasins	48	Calumets	93
Arm-Bands	50	Round Pipestems	94
Dancer's Breechcloths	51	Pipe-Tomahawks	95
Plains Leggins and Breechcloths	52	Pipe Bowls	96
Woodland Leggins and Aprons	53	Fire Coloration	98
Plains Shirts	54	Burnt Etching	99
Buckskin Shirts	55	Fur Tassels	100
Plains Vests and Cuffs	56	Yarn Pompons and Tassels	101
Hair-pipe Breastplates	57	Beading Bands	102
Quill Breastplates and Otters	58	Woodland Beading	104
Plains Clothing (Sioux)	59	Plains Beading	106
Woodland Vests	60	Bags and Pouches—Plains	108
Woodland Clothing (Chippewa)	61	Bags and Pouches—Woodland	109
Plains Dresses and Leggings	62	Decorating Round Sticks	110
Chippewa Dance Dresses	64	Solid Faces	112
Necklaces	66	Body Paint and Tights	114
Dew-claws	68	Wigs	116
Tin-cone Jingles	69	Index	117

ACKNOWLEDGMENTS

THE AUTHOR gratefully expresses his appreciation:
To his friends whose pictures appear in the photographs in this book:

Richard Haller—pages 9, 20, 23, 27, 31, 42, 45 upper right
Robert Meeker—pages x, 37, 41, 45 lower right
Jerry Eha—pages 39, 84
Louis Polk, Jr.—pages 14, 40
James C. Stone—pages 2, 12, 29, 30, 36, 51

Robert Raymond—pages 5, 32, 70

Bemis Avery—pages 25, 45 upper left

John L. Holden—page 45 lower left

Robert Thompson—page 43

George W. Stokes—page 7

John Gamble—page 116

I-in-gi-ge-jig—pages v, ix, 78, 92, 97, 111

To James F. Thompson for his co-operation in taking the photographs on pages 9, 13, 16, 20, 23, 27, 31, 43, 45 (upper right), 46, 48, 61, 96, 103, 105, and 111. To Paul Boris who took the photographs on pages i, 2, 12, 29, 30, 36, 51, and 80. To Arthur C. Allen who took the photographs on pages x, 5, 37, and 70. To Sidney C. McCammon who took the color photograph on the jacket.

To the Bureau of American Ethnology for use of the photograph on page 18. To the Museum of the American Indian, Heye Foundation, for use of the photographs on page 63, and the photograph used as the basis of the sketch on page 62. To the United States Indian Service for use of the photograph on page 76.

To the Great Northern Railway for the use of the photographs on the title page and on pages vii and 107. To the Canadian National Railways for use of the photographs on pages 6 and 67

The following photographs were taken by the author: pages ix, 7, 14, 25, 39, 40, 41, 42, 45 (lower right and upper left), 78, 81, 82, 84, 92, 97.

The Indian items appearing in the following photographs, as well as the majority of those used for the sketches, are or were at one time in the author's possession: i, x, 2, 9, 12, 13, 14, 16, 20, 23, 25, 27, 29, 30, 31, 32, 36, 37, 39, 40, 41, 42, 43, 45, 46, 48, 51, 52, 53, 58, 59, 60, 61, 64, 80, 81, 82, 84, 96, 103, 105, 112, 113.

THE BOOK OF INDIAN-CRAFTS
AND COSTUMES

RIDERS OF THE PLAINS AND ROAMERS OF THE WOODS

IT IS THE INDIANS of the Woodlands and the Plains, more than the others, who have gripped the imagination of the world—the roamers of the northern wildwoods, the wigwam Indians, the masters of woodcraft, the *canoe* Indians; and the riders of the prairies, the tepee Indians, the hunters of buffalo, the *horse* Indians—both vigorous and virile peoples, physically dominant, picturesque in appearance, resplendent in clothing, and romantic in customs. More than from the others, it is from these two groups that this book has drawn its material. The fading of the others somewhat into the background is not due to any lack of regard, but rather to lack of space to give them the prominence that otherwise might be theirs.

In speaking of his crafts, customs and ways of life, it is after all difficult to use the term, *American Indian,* and speak with any degree of accuracy: there are so many tribes, each differing more or less from the next. But while the tribes of the country, taken as a whole, may differ, those living in the same general area are very much alike in their customs. Because of this tendency of *neighboring* tribes to resemble each other, the Indians of North America divide themselves into areas of resemblance, or *cultural areas.* Of these there are seven: (1) *Eastern and Northern Woodland,* (2) *Plains,* (3) *Southwest,* (4) *Southeastern,* (5) *Pacific Northwest,* (6) *Plateau,* and (7) *California.*

Rather than of tribes, therefore, it is of the cultural areas that this book usually speaks. During the days when the Indians were being herded on reservations, Oklahoma was made the dumping ground of many tribes from several cultural areas, with the result that a hodgepodge of cultural patterns existed there in close proximity, and naturally became somewhat intermingled. The crafts that have characterized this area since that time are spoken of in this book as *Oklahoma* for the sake of convenience and brevity.

I like Indians of whatever area—I like their ways, their outlook on life, their romantic disposition, their indwelling artistic spirit, their capacity to see beauty in the commonplace, to create beauty from the commonplace. This pursuit of beauty as a life goal comes as a bright ray of sunshine in the gray dullness of our own materialism. We have much to give them, but they have much to give us. Their dances I have presented in another book, *Dances and Stories of the American Indian;* their crafts are the subject of the present volume. From these crafts I hope will come not only that depth of satisfaction that stems from working with primitive things in the primitive way, but something of that beauty-seeking attitude which made life richer for the Indian, and can make it richer for us.

WAR-BONNET

THE MOST PICTURESQUE HAT ever worn—such is the eagle-feather war-bonnet of the Sioux. Yes, of the *Sioux,* for it was their's and their's alone in those good old days when the buffalo roamed and men were free. But nowadays it is the possession of all the tribes, taken over by them not because of its beauty alone, but because the wearing of it is expected of them. It has become a sort of symbol of things Indian, so much so that in the white man's eyes, an Indian without a war-bonnet is scarcely an Indian at all.

It is good to own a war-bonnet, good to make one, especially if it be of white-and-black-tipped eagle feathers. For there is medicine in these beautiful, reserved and dignified quills—medicine that becomes the possession of all who work with them. One is never quite the same after dealing with eagle feathers—they do something to the spirit.

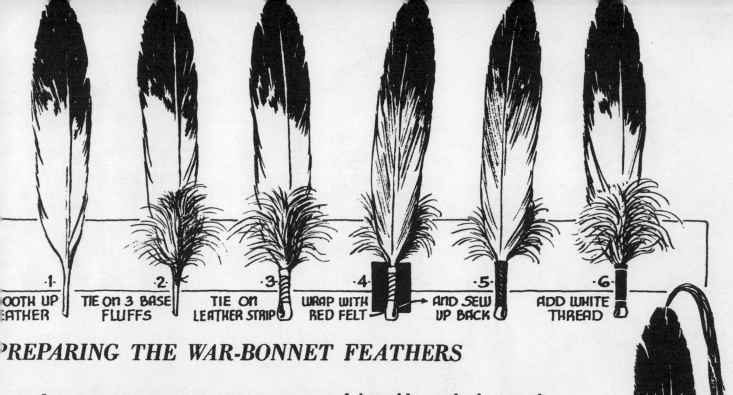

OOTH UP   TIE ON 3 BASE   TIE ON   WRAP WITH   AND SEW   ADD WHITE
EATHER   FLUFFS   LEATHER STRIP   RED FELT   UP BACK   THREAD

PREPARING THE WAR-BONNET FEATHERS

IT IS THE WHITE-AND-BLACK TAIL FEATHERS of the golden eagle that are the war-bonnet feathers, the *coup feathers* of the Plains Redmen. The more white on them the more highly they are regarded. As second choice, use dark eagle quills, mottled if possible but all dark if necessary. Imitation white eagle feathers are on the market for the purpose. Get the best you can find, but make a headdress, even though it be of turkey feathers.

Thirty-two feathers are needed, half curving to the right and half to the left. Two should be larger and nearly straight for the center feathers. And all should match, which is to say they should be uniform and look well together. In addition the following are needed, best obtained from an Indian-craft supply company:

·7·

GLUE RED
HORSEHAIR
TO TIP

96 white base fluffies   32 pieces red felt, 1½ by 2½ inches
32 smaller tip fluffies   red or white horsehair
32 leather strips ⅛ by 4½ inches   leather thong
                                      airplane glue

Following the numbers on the drawings, proceed as follows:

1. Smooth up the feathers by fingering it. If in bad shape, steam it first.

2. Tie a cluster of three fluffies at the base with thread and then add glue. *Good Indian taste demands that base fluffies be white.*

3. Fold a leather strip over the base and wrap securely, leaving just enough space at the bottom to slip a thong through. This leather should lie in the same plane as the web of the feather.

4. Wrap the felt around the quill, and (5) sew up the back.

6. Wrap with white thread as shown for ornamentation.

7. Glue about a dozen strands of horsehair to the tip.

8. Glue a tip fluffy (white, yellow, or red) over the horsehair.

·8·

GLUE TIP
FLUFF OVER
HORSEHAIR

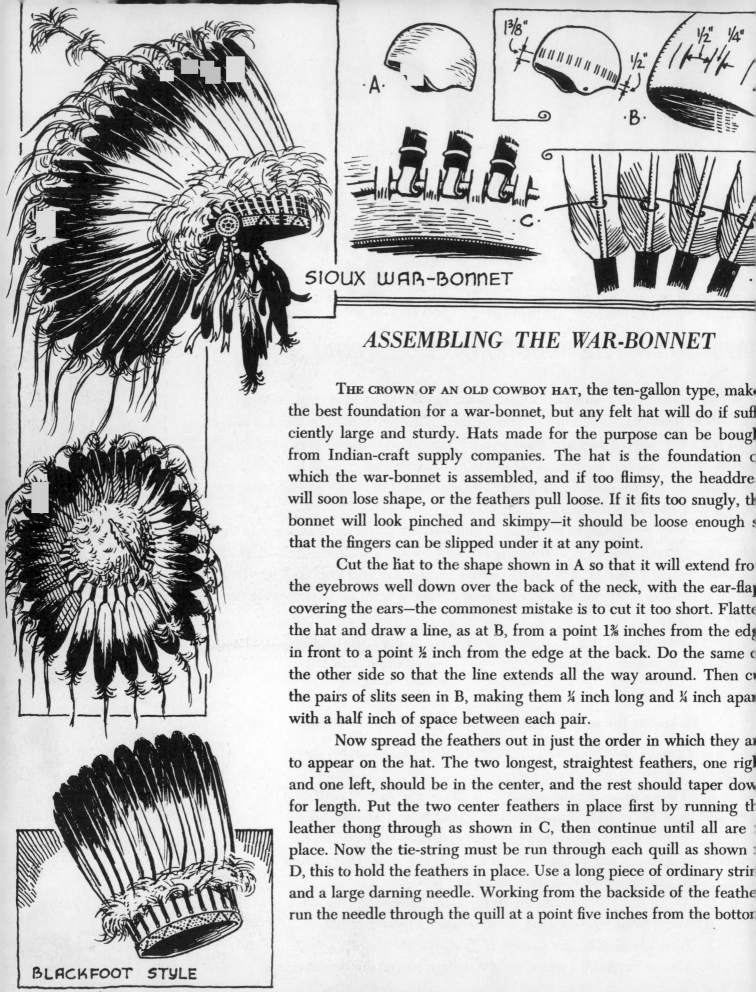

SIOUX WAR-BONNET

BLACKFOOT STYLE

ASSEMBLING THE WAR-BONNET

THE CROWN OF AN OLD COWBOY HAT, the ten-gallon type, make
the best foundation for a war-bonnet, but any felt hat will do if suff
ciently large and sturdy. Hats made for the purpose can be bough
from Indian-craft supply companies. The hat is the foundation o
which the war-bonnet is assembled, and if too flimsy, the headdre
will soon lose shape, or the feathers pull loose. If it fits too snugly, th
bonnet will look pinched and skimpy—it should be loose enough s
that the fingers can be slipped under it at any point.

Cut the hat to the shape shown in A so that it will extend fro
the eyebrows well down over the back of the neck, with the ear-fla
covering the ears—the commonest mistake is to cut it too short. Flatte
the hat and draw a line, as at B, from a point 1⅜ inches from the edg
in front to a point ½ inch from the edge at the back. Do the same o
the other side so that the line extends all the way around. Then c
the pairs of slits seen in B, making them ¼ inch long and ¼ inch apa
with a half inch of space between each pair.

Now spread the feathers out in just the order in which they a
to appear on the hat. The two longest, straightest feathers, one rig
and one left, should be in the center, and the rest should taper dow
for length. Put the two center feathers in place first by running th
leather thong through as shown in C, then continue until all are
place. Now the tie-string must be run through each quill as shown
D, this to hold the feathers in place. Use a long piece of ordinary strir
and a large darning needle. Working from the backside of the feathe
run the needle through the quill at a point five inches from the botton

then loop it and run it through again as in D so that the feather cannot slip. Start at the center feathers and work both ways so that the ends of the string are tied at the back.

Sew the beaded browband across the front, or as a substitute, a band of colored cloth as the Indian has done on page 6. Beaded browbands are 12 inches long and 1 to 1½ inches wide. Usually the beaded band is terminated by a round beaded rosette at each end.

THE MAJOR PLUME

THE MAJOR PLUME which extends out from the middle of the war-bonnet behind (page 4) is more than mere ornamentation—it identifies the owner of the headdress. And so no two are just alike. It is made from a spiked eagle wing feather 20 or more inches long, from which the web has been stripped as shown. A piece of wire may be used as a substitute. Wrap the stripped quill with colored ribbon or yarn, tie and glue a bunch of six fluffies of any color to the tip, and another clump of fluffies near its middle. Slit the bottom end of the quill and tuck the end up inside to form a loop, and sew this loop to the hat a little front of center. Cover the back of the hat completely with white fluffies sewed to the felt.

Side hangings attached at the ends of the beaded band and hanging down over the shoulder add greatly to the bonnet's attractiveness. These may be of ermine tails, whole weasel skins, any white fur, colored ribbons, or a feather.

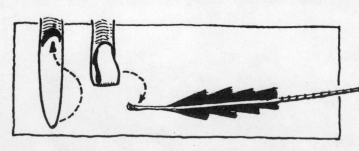

MAJOR PLUME

6

SETTING THE WAR-BONNET

WHEN IT IS ALL ASSEMBLED, the time has come to "set" the war-bonnet so as to form a perfectly balanced, uniform spread. Note the beautiful crest on the otherwise barren headdress on the opposite page, spreading out magnificently from the two perfect center feathers. When placed on someone's head the bonnet may appear too loose, too pinched, lop-sided, or sagging in spots, all of which can be remedied by shifting the feathers a little this way or that, first loosening the string that holds each in place. Study the sides as well as the front—each feather should overlap the bottom edge of the feather above it to form the beautiful side view seen on page 2. Feathers vary, and so no two headdresses can be set so as to give exactly the same spread. If the feathers simply will not stand out nicely, "rats" such as women use in their hair may be tucked under the quills from behind to hold them out.

If the war-bonnet collapses or turns inside out when the head is bent forward, the feathers should be shoved closer together and the tie-string shortened.

TASSELS OF WHITE FUR

SIDE HANGINGS   HAWK FEATHERS   RIBBONS   ERMINE TAILS

7

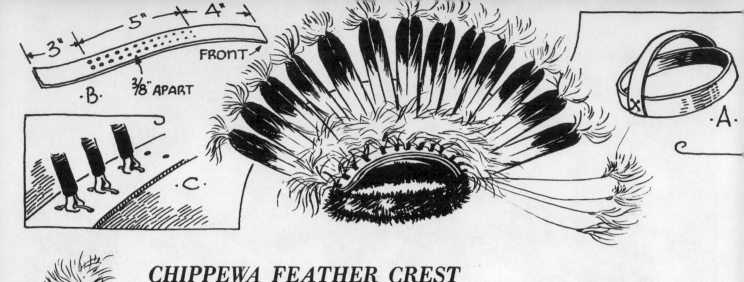

CHIPPEWA FEATHER CREST

HERE IS A HEADDRESS of great charm and effectiveness. A favorite of the long ago, it is not seen so often nowadays, but it is nevertheless the only eagle-feather headdress suitable for a dancer. War-bonnets are appropriate on wrinkled old chiefs but are unbecoming and cumbersome on dashing dancers.

Thirteen eagle tail feathers make the crest, six rights and seven lefts. As a second choice, spiked wing feathers cut down to 12 inches were used, and even barred chicken feathers are effective. The feathers are prepared as for the war-bonnet (page 3) except that fluffies are added to *both* sides since both sides are visible, and the leather loop is placed at right angles to the web as at D.

To make the crest in the ancient way, make a leather strap foundation (A) to fit the head, then prepare another strap (B) of thin black leather to carry the feathers, punching holes in it with an awl following the dimensions shown. Attach the feathers with string as in C, placing the six rights in front and the seven lefts in back. Then run a tie-string through the quills as in making a war-bonnet. Attach the strap with the feathers to the top strap of the foundation, using string so that it can easily be removed for packing. Stretch the tie-string very tight and tie the ends front and back to the foundation. The tie-string thus pulls the feathers erect, yet permits them to wave in the breeze with the dancer's movements, giving the crest a wild primitive flavor. The circular leather strap should be covered with fur (the Chippewas used beaver), red cloth, or a beaded band.

A modern method of construction is shown at the bottom of the page. Cut two pieces of tin exactly the same size, to the shape shown at E. Cut a piece of buckskin to the same shape but an inch larger, and stretch

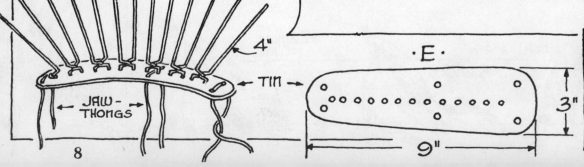

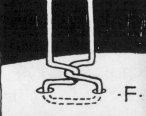

8

it tightly over one of the pieces of tin, gluing the overlapping edges to the backside—the buckskin side rests on the head. Place the two pieces of tin together and punch the holes shown in E through both. Then put the wires in place as shown at F. Clip off the bottoms of the quills and slip the feathers on the wires. The crest is used with a wig and held by jaw-thongs.

A fascinating touch on headgear of this type are the antennae of white fluffies extending out in front, made of very fine wire which becomes invisible at a few feet, giving the fluffies the appearance of floating in air.

WIRE ANTENNAE

BARRED FEATHERS

RT
E WING
KES

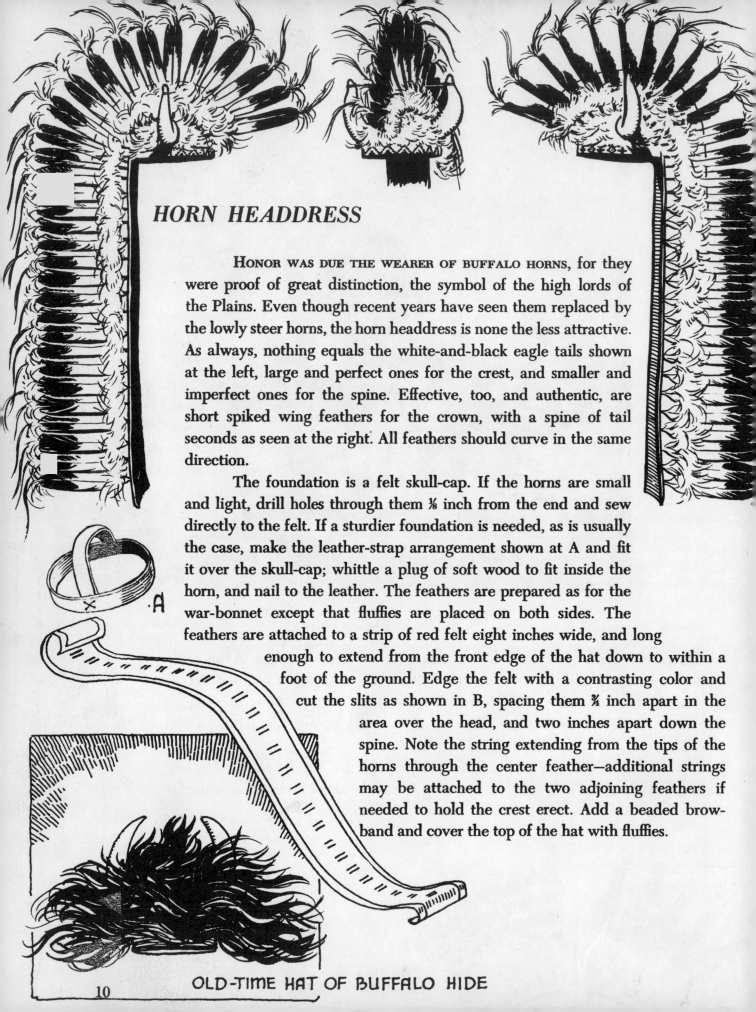

HORN HEADDRESS

HONOR WAS DUE THE WEARER OF BUFFALO HORNS, for they were proof of great distinction, the symbol of the high lords of the Plains. Even though recent years have seen them replaced by the lowly steer horns, the horn headdress is none the less attractive. As always, nothing equals the white-and-black eagle tails shown at the left, large and perfect ones for the crest, and smaller and imperfect ones for the spine. Effective, too, and authentic, are short spiked wing feathers for the crown, with a spine of tail seconds as seen at the right. All feathers should curve in the same direction.

The foundation is a felt skull-cap. If the horns are small and light, drill holes through them ⅛ inch from the end and sew directly to the felt. If a sturdier foundation is needed, as is usually the case, make the leather-strap arrangement shown at A and fit it over the skull-cap; whittle a plug of soft wood to fit inside the horn, and nail to the leather. The feathers are prepared as for the war-bonnet except that fluffies are placed on both sides. The feathers are attached to a strip of red felt eight inches wide, and long enough to extend from the front edge of the hat down to within a foot of the ground. Edge the felt with a contrasting color and cut the slits as shown in B, spacing them ¾ inch apart in the area over the head, and two inches apart down the spine. Note the string extending from the tips of the horns through the center feather—additional strings may be attached to the two adjoining feathers if needed to hold the crest erect. Add a beaded brow-band and cover the top of the hat with fluffies.

OLD-TIME HAT OF BUFFALO HIDE

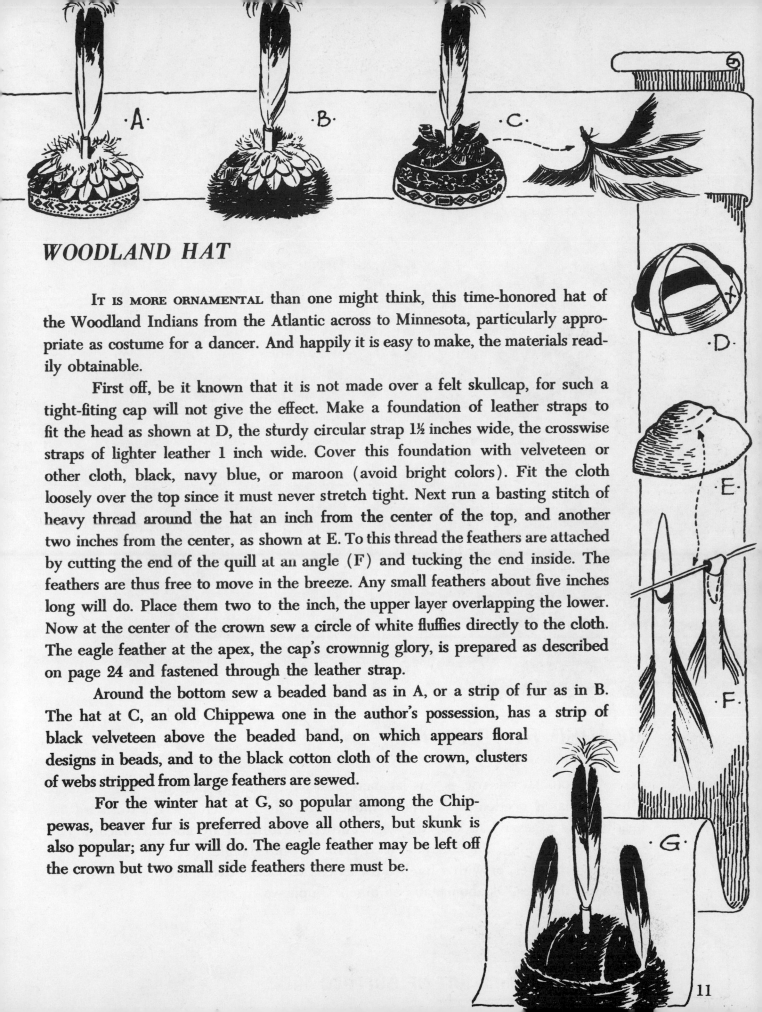

WOODLAND HAT

IT IS MORE ORNAMENTAL than one might think, this time-honored hat of the Woodland Indians from the Atlantic across to Minnesota, particularly appropriate as costume for a dancer. And happily it is easy to make, the materials readily obtainable.

First off, be it known that it is not made over a felt skullcap, for such a tight-fiting cap will not give the effect. Make a foundation of leather straps to fit the head as shown at D, the sturdy circular strap 1½ inches wide, the crosswise straps of lighter leather 1 inch wide. Cover this foundation with velveteen or other cloth, black, navy blue, or maroon (avoid bright colors). Fit the cloth loosely over the top since it must never stretch tight. Next run a basting stitch of heavy thread around the hat an inch from the center of the top, and another two inches from the center, as shown at E. To this thread the feathers are attached by cutting the end of the quill at an angle (F) and tucking the end inside. The feathers are thus free to move in the breeze. Any small feathers about five inches long will do. Place them two to the inch, the upper layer overlapping the lower. Now at the center of the crown sew a circle of white fluffies directly to the cloth. The eagle feather at the apex, the cap's crownnig glory, is prepared as described on page 24 and fastened through the leather strap.

Around the bottom sew a beaded band as in A, or a strip of fur as in B. The hat at C, an old Chippewa one in the author's possession, has a strip of black velveteen above the beaded band, on which appears floral designs in beads, and to the black cotton cloth of the crown, clusters of webs stripped from large feathers are sewed.

For the winter hat at G, so popular among the Chippewas, beaver fur is preferred above all others, but skunk is also popular; any fur will do. The eagle feather may be left off the crown but two small side feathers there must be.

11

BEADED HEADBANDS

So CHARACTERISTIC IS THE BEADED BROWBAND that its presence alone is often all that is needed for a typical Indian head effect. When a wig is worn, a headband is necessary to keep the wig in order. Headbands are about 1¼ inches wide, 18 inches long. They may be used plain, or with dangles over the temples or circling the eyes, or with a forehead rosette. The bottom two in the photograph are Plains, the next Oklahoma, and all others Chippewa.

FOREHEAD ROSETTES

Nothing ornaments a headband for dancing garb so effectively as a rosette in the middle of the forehead. These brilliant little circles of color catch the eye irresistibly and seem to highlight the dancer's whole personality.

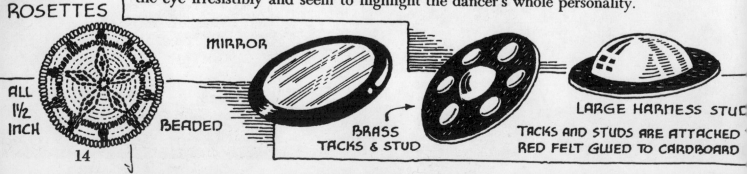

CENTER ROSETTES

MIRROR

ALL 1½ INCH

BEADED

BRASS TACKS & STUD

LARGE HARNESS STUD

TACKS AND STUDS ARE ATTACHED RED FELT GLUED TO CARDBOARD

14

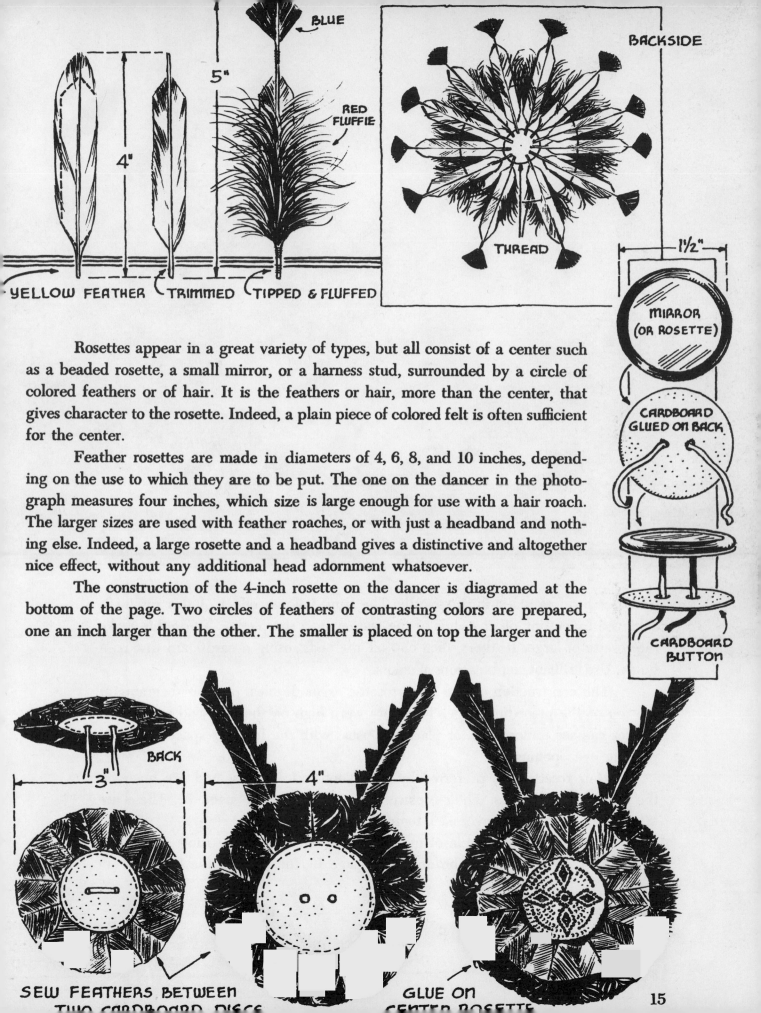

BLUE

5"

RED FLUFFIE

YELLOW FEATHER · TRIMMED · TIPPED & FLUFFED

BACKSIDE

THREAD

1½"

MIRROR (OR ROSETTE)

CARDBOARD GLUED ON BACK

CARDBOARD BUTTON

Rosettes appear in a great variety of types, but all consist of a center such as a beaded rosette, a small mirror, or a harness stud, surrounded by a circle of colored feathers or of hair. It is the feathers or hair, more than the center, that gives character to the rosette. Indeed, a plain piece of colored felt is often sufficient for the center.

Feather rosettes are made in diameters of 4, 6, 8, and 10 inches, depending on the use to which they are to be put. The one on the dancer in the photograph measures four inches, which size is large enough for use with a hair roach. The larger sizes are used with feather roaches, or with just a headband and nothing else. Indeed, a large rosette and a headband gives a distinctive and altogether nice effect, without any additional head adornment whatsoever.

The construction of the 4-inch rosette on the dancer is diagramed at the bottom of the page. Two circles of feathers of contrasting colors are prepared, one an inch larger than the other. The smaller is placed on top the larger and the

BACK

3"

4"

SEW FEATHERS BETWEEN TWO CARDBOARD PIECE

GLUE ON CENTER ROSETTE

15

center of beading glued in the middle. The trim, tailored effect of this rosette is achieved by cutting off the ends of the feathers to a sharp edge. To do this, make the rosette of larger feathers, then clip off the ends, using a cardboard disc as a guide. Use brilliant combinations of colors.

The construction of the large rosettes is made clear by the diagrams at the top of the preceding page. These are worn high on the forehead so that the wearer can see underneath, or placed as usual with the feathers spaced so as to provide eye openings.

Hair rosettes are preferred by the Woodland Indians, and are made in the same range of sizes. Their construction is described on page 28. These are often worn in pairs, one over each temple.

Rosettes are also made of mercerized embroidery floss, using a one-inch fringe of it, as seen on the headband on page 13, fourth from the top.

ROSETTE
DESIGNS

BLACKFOOT   N. WOODLAND   OKLAHOMA   PLAINS

TURBANS AND HAIR FEATHERS

THE INTERESTING turban worn by this dignified old Chippewa is made of a strip of beaver fur folded and sewed. Skunk, although less prized, is also used to make turbans of black striped with white. Another common type is a round roll of padding an inch thick covered with buckskin. The feathers are set in tubes to permit movement (see page 24). The rakish look of these turbans, giving the wearer distinctive style and character, results from the movement of the feathers,

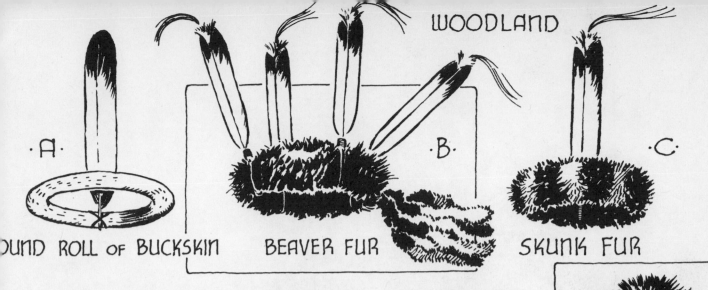

WOODLAND

·A·

ROUND ROLL of BUCKSKIN

·B·

BEAVER FUR

·C·

SKUNK FUR

·D·

causing them to assume interesting and constantly changing angles. Cover the tubes with fur to match.

An interesting style in beaded headbands, common on the Plains, is shown at the lower left corner, in which the beading is placed across the *back* of the head, and tied with a slender thong across the forehead. These are often worn with rosettes of the cut-out type as shown, made either of beading or of light-colored rawhide. Such rosettes are also used separately as hair ornaments, fluffs attached to them, and tied to the hair.

Feathers for the hair are attached to wooden pegs about half the thickness of a pencil, and stuck in the hair. Not only feathers, but stripped quills adorned with fluffs, and slender strips of rawhide fluff-tipped and wrapped with yarn, are used in this way. On the Plains the pegs are sometimes inserted into a beaded hanging tied to the back of the head and extending down the neck, at the bottom of which the hair of a bull's tail is attached—this is called a *wapeginicki*. The beading measures two by nine inches.

PEG FITS HERE

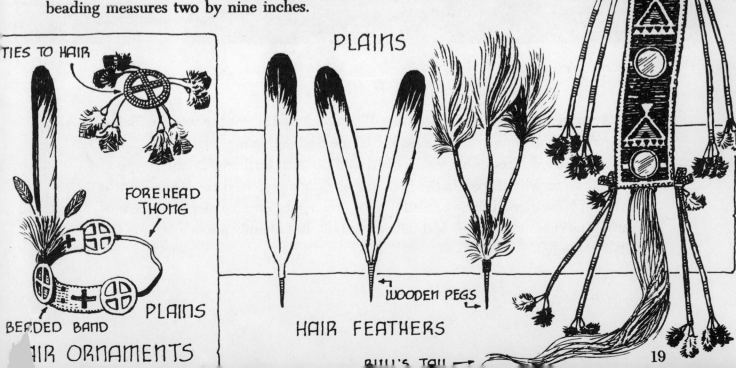

TIES TO HAIR

FOREHEAD THONG

BEADED BAND

PLAINS

HAIR ORNAMENTS

PLAINS

HAIR FEATHERS

WOODEN PEGS

BULL'S TAIL

19

HAIR ROACH

IT WAS THE SAME throughout the Woodlands and across the western Plains: the hair roach was the coveted headdress of the dashing young men in the dance. Only the wrinkled faces of old men looked well beneath feathered bonnets; men of youth and vigor who leaped to the booming of drums preferred the roach. So it is to this day, even though these beautiful head ornaments, once so plentiful, are now becoming increasingly scarce—and difficult to buy. But happily a roach of sorts can be readily made.

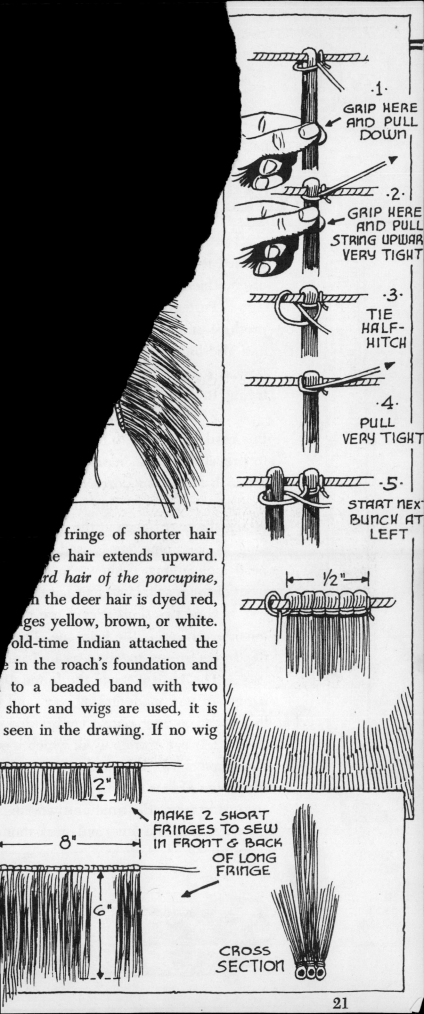

·1·
GRIP HERE
AND PULL
DOWN

·2·
GRIP HERE
AND PULL
STRING UPWAR
VERY TIGHT

·3·
TIE
HALF-
HITCH

·4·
PULL
VERY TIGHT

·5·
START NEX
BUNCH AT
LEFT

½"

fringe of shorter hair
  hair extends upward.
rd hair of the porcupine,
  the deer hair is dyed red,
  ges yellow, brown, or white.
  old-time Indian attached the
  in the roach's foundation and
  to a beaded band with two
  short and wigs are used, it is
  seen in the drawing. If no wig

2"

8"

MAKE 2 SHORT
FRINGES TO SEW
IN FRONT & BACK
OF LONG
FRINGE

6"

CROSS
SECTION

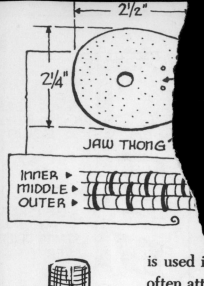

INNER ▸
MIDDLE ▸
OUTER ▸

2½"

2¼"

JAW THONG

← 1"

·D·

WRAP
ROACH
ON STICK
WHEN
NOT IN
USE

is used it

often attac

Porcup

produce enough

and also binder t

typical roach when

trying to imitate th

First attach thr

this cord the hair is to

to prevent it from slippi

a bunch of about a dozen

middle over the cord, thus m

attach the next bunch at the

long. If porcupine hair is used,

be 8 inches long as shown in

front of the roach. Horsehair not t

Now two short fringes are n

outside and inside the long one. The

the three fringes together as indicate

The Indians made the foundatic

fringes of hair made in this way, and t

like effect; in later years they braided c

from a felt hat is often used, which met

the shape shown at A and sew togethe

the fringe of hair to it by sewing the in

at C, starting at the front and working

Attach the jaw- and neck-thong

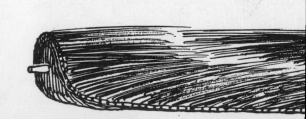

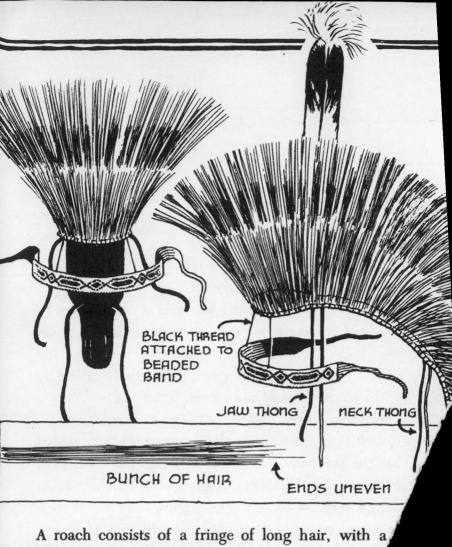

BLACK THREAD
ATTACHED TO
BEADED
BAND

JAW THONG   NECK THONG

BUNCH OF HAIR

ENDS UNEVEN

A roach consists of a fringe of long hair, with a
ther side of it, all attached to a foundation so that th
lmost universally the long fringe is made of the *gua*
nd the short fringes of *deer tail*. On the typical roac
ut occasionally roaches are seen with the short frin

It was by means of his long hair that the
ach to his head, running a lock through the hole
notting it. And in front he attached the roach
rands of black thread. Nowadays, when hair
est attached by jaw-thongs and neck-thongs

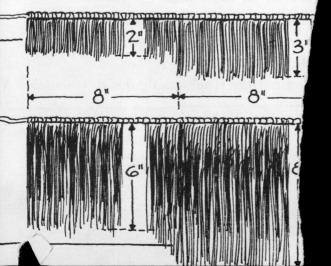

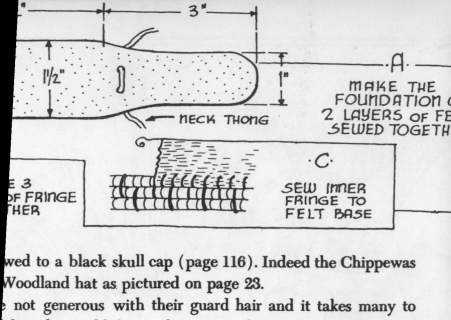

...wed to a black skull cap (page 116). Indeed the Chippewas ...Woodland hat as pictured on page 23.

...e not generous with their guard hair and it takes many to ...l horsehair sold for craft use may be used as a substitute, ...e unravelled and dyed red. The general color effect of the ...viewed from a distance is red anyway, and little is gained by ...e tan and black porcupine hair—make it all red.

...ce feet of ¹⁄₁₆-inch cord tightly between two uprights. To ...e tied with heavy linen or button thread, heavily waxed ...g. Tie the thread to the cord as shown at Figure 1. Take ...hairs measuring 12 inches long, double the hair at its ...aking it 6 inches long, and tie as shown at 2 and 3; then ...eft, and continue thus until the fringe is 24 inches ...the hair in the middle section of the fringe should ...he drawing, this longer center section to be the ...o stand erect if longer than 6 inches.

...ade in the same way, 2 to 3 inches long, to go ...inner fringe may be omitted if need be. Sew ...ed at B.

...on for the roach by sewing together many ...hen clipping the hair short to give a cloth-...rd into a foundation. But nowadays felt ...od is by far the easiest. Cut two pieces to ...making a double thickness. Then attach ...r layer of the fringe to the felt as shown ...ck.

...nd put the roach on the head, placing

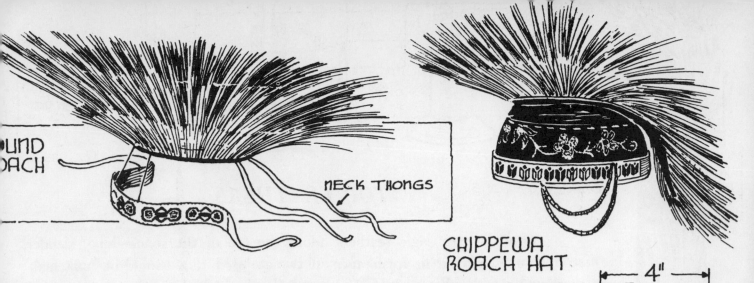

ROUND ROACH

NECK THONGS

CHIPPEWA ROACH HAT

4"

FOUNDATION FOR ROUND ROACH

it as in the photograph. Put the beaded band on and then run the two strands of heavy black thread from roach to headband, and tie at just the proper length.

Made as described, we have a full-sized roach extending well down over the neck. A shorter one covering the head only can be made on a base 6 inches long, requiring only 14 inches of fringe. Indeed, the Indians often used *round* roaches as a topknot only, with 12 inches of fringe on a circular foundation.

Roaches must be handled very carefully so as not to break the hairs or warp them. When not in use, the roach should be carefully wrapped over a stick made as shown. With the stick in place, wet the hands and smooth the hairs carefully, then bandage the entire length with strips of cloth. The roach should be frequently combed out with a wet comb.

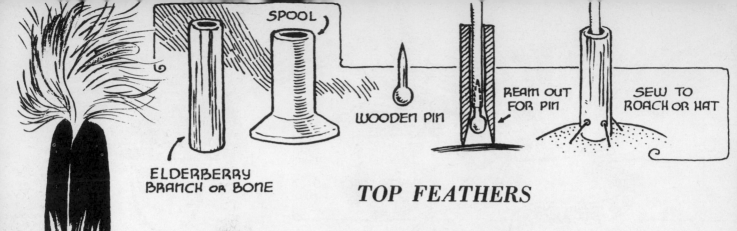

ELDERBERRY
BRANCH OR BONE

WOODEN PIN

REAM OUT
FOR PIN

SEW TO
ROACH OR HAT

SPOOL

TOP FEATHERS

ONE OR TWO eagle feathers adorn the top of the roach—long, slender, straight ones, perfect in appearance. If two are used, they should be "matched," duplicating each other in shape and mottling, of which those in the photograph are excellent examples. A certain shape is sought, so characteristic of roaches that feathers of this type are often spoken of as roach feathers. The unintiated is often at a loss to know how to obtain these just-right quills. The secret, as any old Plains Indian will tell you, is that the two *outside* feathers from an eagle's tail are used. Those from the same bird will usually be "matched." Any good straight feathers can of course be used.

The feather is set in a tube about a half inch wide and two inches long, which, in the old days, was usually made of bone. A branch of elderberry is the quickest source, from which the pithy center is reamed out. In modern style, a spool can be cut down as shown.

The important thing is that the feather be free to rotate in the tube, so as to spin and twirl in the breeze or with the dancer's movements. There are three ways that this is done:

1. Easiest is the method shown at A: Drill a tiny hole through the tube a half inch from the bottom, insert the feather in the tube and, using a darning needle, run a string through the tube and the shaft of the feather. Leave the string loose so that it will sag as shown, and wrap the ends around the tube and tie. If the string is drawn tight, the feather cannot move.

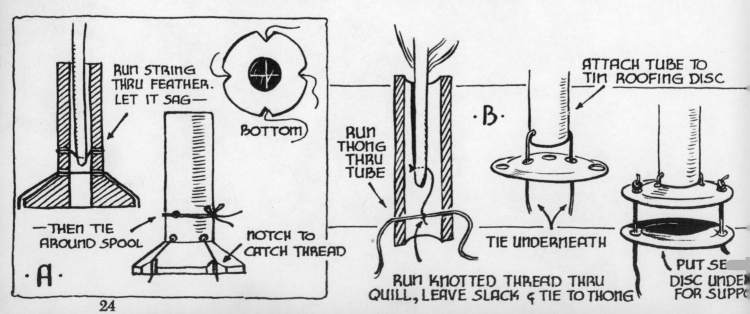

RUN STRING
THRU FEATHER.
LET IT SAG—

BOTTOM

—THEN TIE
AROUND SPOOL

·A·

NOTCH TO
CATCH THREAD

RUN
THONG
THRU
TUBE

·B·

RUN KNOTTED THREAD THRU
QUILL, LEAVE SLACK & TIE TO THONG

TIE UNDERNEATH

ATTACH TUBE TO
TIN ROOFING DISC

PUT SE
DISC UNDE
FOR SUPPO

2.   Better in that it permits more twirling is the method at B. Run a buck-skin thong through the tube and tie the feather to it with heavy linen thread, leaving at least a half inch of slack. The end of the quill should be first wrapped with fine thread to prevent splitting.

3.   In the old days the method shown at the top of page 24 was more common. Whittle a little ball-headed pin of hardwood, ream out the bottom end of the tube to accommodate the head of the pin, and insert. Clip off the end of the quill and force it over the pin. The feather thus can be removed for packing.

A spool is easily attached to the roach as shown at A. If a straight tube is used, attach it to a tin roofing disc as seen at B. A second disc underneath the roach will help to hold it rigid.

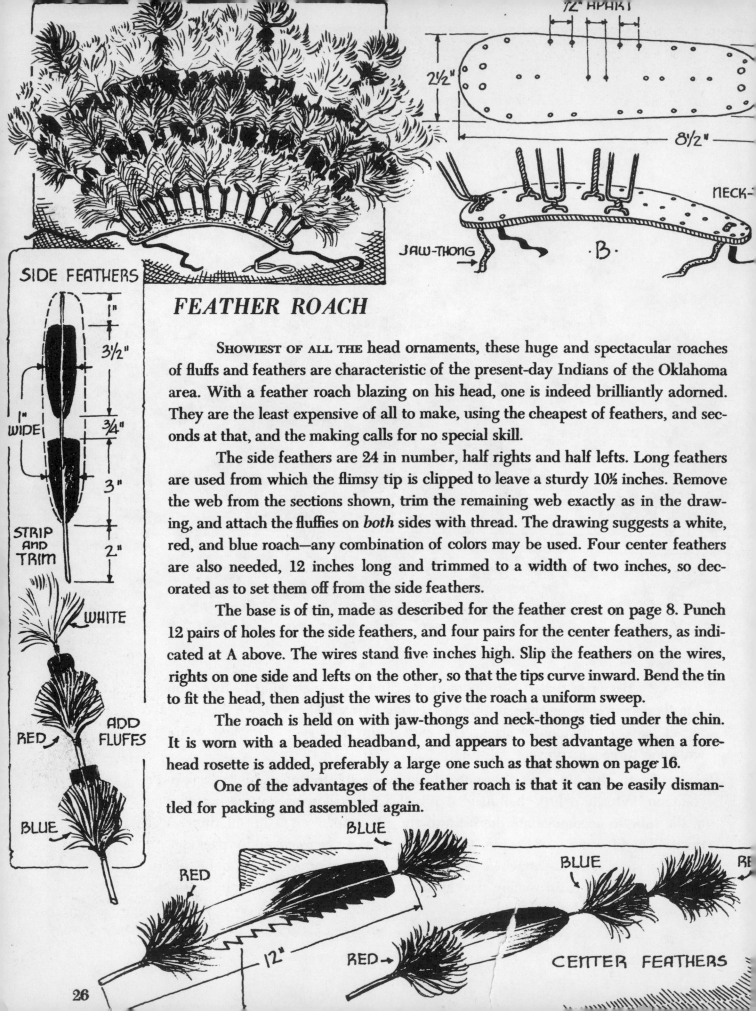

SIDE FEATHERS

1"

3½"

1" WIDE

¾"

3"

STRIP AND TRIM

2"

WHITE

RED

ADD FLUFFS

BLUE

2½"

½" APART

8½"

NECK-

JAW-THONG

·B·

FEATHER ROACH

SHOWIEST OF ALL THE head ornaments, these huge and spectacular roaches of fluffs and feathers are characteristic of the present-day Indians of the Oklahoma area. With a feather roach blazing on his head, one is indeed brilliantly adorned. They are the least expensive of all to make, using the cheapest of feathers, and seconds at that, and the making calls for no special skill.

The side feathers are 24 in number, half rights and half lefts. Long feathers are used from which the flimsy tip is clipped to leave a sturdy 10½ inches. Remove the web from the sections shown, trim the remaining web exactly as in the drawing, and attach the fluffies on *both* sides with thread. The drawing suggests a white, red, and blue roach—any combination of colors may be used. Four center feathers are also needed, 12 inches long and trimmed to a width of two inches, so decorated as to set them off from the side feathers.

The base is of tin, made as described for the feather crest on page 8. Punch 12 pairs of holes for the side feathers, and four pairs for the center feathers, as indicated at A above. The wires stand five inches high. Slip the feathers on the wires, rights on one side and lefts on the other, so that the tips curve inward. Bend the tin to fit the head, then adjust the wires to give the roach a uniform sweep.

The roach is held on with jaw-thongs and neck-thongs tied under the chin. It is worn with a beaded headband, and appears to best advantage when a forehead rosette is added, preferably a large one such as that shown on page 16.

One of the advantages of the feather roach is that it can be easily dismantled for packing and assembled again.

BLUE

RED

BLUE

RE

BLUE

12"

RED→

CENTER FEATHERS

HAIR BUSTLES AND ROSETTES

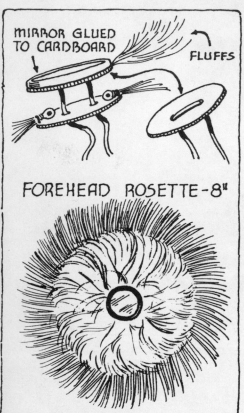

MIRROR GLUED TO CARDBOARD

FLUFFS

FOREHEAD ROSETTE - 8"

WE SEE THE HAIR BUSTLE on the wrist of the dancer in the photograph. It is made of horsehair dyed red (in the absence of porcupine hair) and measures about 13 inches across. The hair is tied as described for making a roach on page 21. Only 4 inches of hair fringe is needed for each bustle. Use 10-inch horsehair, about 18 strands to a bunch, arrange it so that the ends are uneven, and double it over the cord so that the one end is 6 inches long and the other 4½ inches. This makes the bustle thicker in the middle than at the edges. When the fringe is completed bend it into a circle and sew to a 2-inch disc of felt. Sew a buckskin thong to the bottom of the disc as a tie-thong, and glue a mirror on the top side with airplane glue.

Bustles of this type made 20 inches in diameter are effective at the shoulders. Smaller ones 10 inches in diameter make excellent rosettes for an armband just above the elbow.

Most popular are the little hair rosettes worn on the beaded headband in the middle of the forehead, or to one side just in front of the temple (see photograph on page 16). These are often worn in pairs, one over each temple. They are 8 inches in diameter and are made thinner, using only 8 or 10 hairs to a bunch. In this case double the hair over the cord at its middle so that both ends are the same length, and attach a circle of small fluffies around the mirror in the middle. The fluffies are sewed or glued to a cardboard disc, and the mirror is glued on top as shown in the drawing.

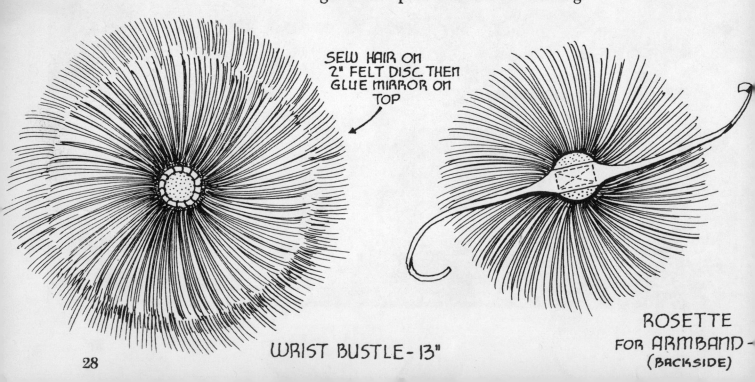

SEW HAIR ON 2" FELT DISC THEN GLUE MIRROR ON TOP

WRIST BUSTLE - 13"

ROSETTE FOR ARMBAND (BACKSIDE)

FEATHER BUSTLES

IN NO OTHER WAY can a man adorn himself for the dance so brilliantly or appropriately: *bustles*—big circles of feathers and color, pointing up shoulders and filling the back with vivid splendor! They are clothing aplenty for lithe and flowing muscles, without which one feels himself quite out of mood and character. From the feathery Sioux types to the tailored Oklahoma styles and the flaming sunbursts, they are one and all startling in vividness and resplendent with atmosphere. And happily, no item of feather equipment is so easy and interesting to make. Their story rightly occupies the next several pages.

SIOUX BUSTLES

TYPICAL SIOUX BUSTLES appear on the dancer above. They consist of about five circles of feathers stacked one on top of the other, plus a rosette of fluffies in the center. Such bustles are usually worn in sets of three. Any and all types of feathers may be used, the bustle in the diagram being made entirely of chicken feathers, barred and white. Hawk and owl feathers are ideal.

To make the tail bustle, 16 10-inch feathers are needed for the first layer. Strip the web down with the fingers, one-third the length of the feather as illustrated, and glue a fluffy to the tip with airplane glue. Cut the end of the shaft at an angle as at A and tuck the end up inside to make a loop. Run a string through the loops of all 16 feathers and tie it so as to hold them in a circle. Then run a tie-string through the feathers farther out to keep the circle spread. The other layers are made in the same way, using feathers of the size and type illustrated.

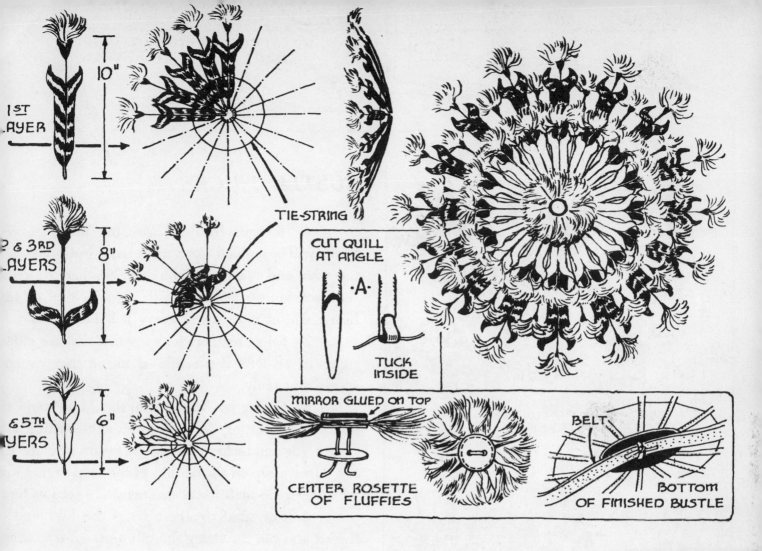

1ST LAYER — 10"

2 & 3RD LAYERS — 8"

4 & 5TH LAYERS — 6"

TIE-STRING

CUT QUILL AT ANGLE · A · TUCK INSIDE

MIRROR GLUED ON TOP

CENTER ROSETTE OF FLUFFIES

BELT

BOTTOM OF FINISHED BUSTLE

To make the center rosette, arrange 16 fluffies between two cardboard discs and either sew or glue the discs together. Punch two holes through the discs for the tie-thong and glue a mirror on top. Stack the various layers in order, place the rosette in the middle, and run the tie-thongs through the centers of all layers. Cut out the top of a tin-can for a bottom button, punch two holes in it and run the tie-thongs through and tie tightly. For a belt to tie around the waist, use a strip of cloth two inches wide.

The arm bustles differ only in size, the feathers in the various rows being 8, 7, and 5 inches respectively.

The tip fluffies on each row should be of a different color, and the fluffies in the center can be of any color desired, or of mixed colors. By using different colors of feathers and fluffies, bustles in infinite variety can be made. Similarly, great variety can be achieved in the center rosettes.

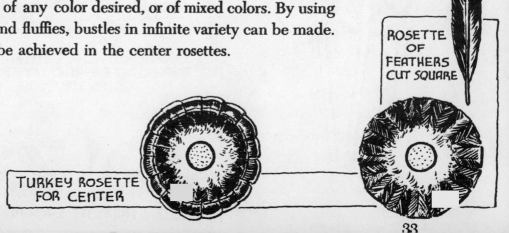

TURKEY ROSETTE FOR CENTER

ROSETTE OF FEATHERS CUT SQUARE

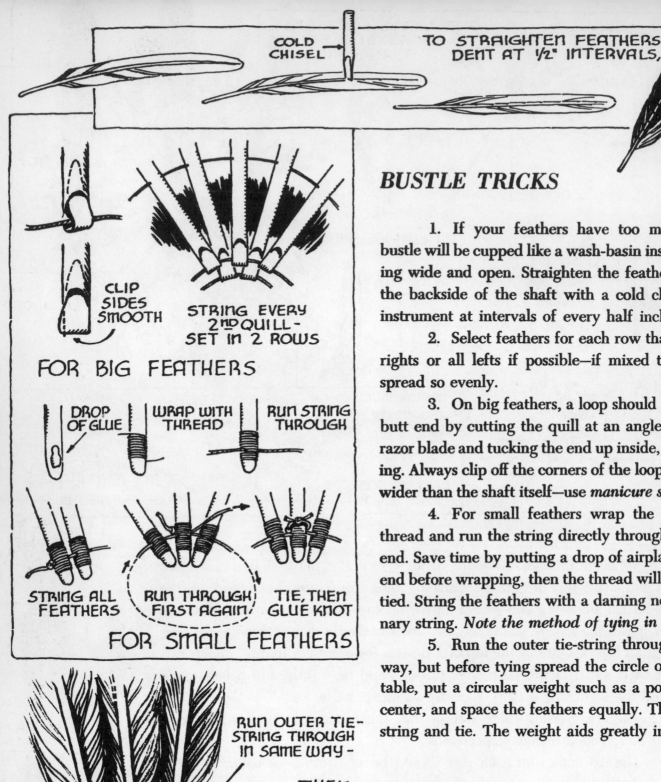

COLD CHISEL →

TO STRAIGHTEN FEATHERS DENT AT ½" INTERVALS,

CLIP SIDES SMOOTH

STRING EVERY 2ND QUILL – SET IN 2 ROWS

FOR BIG FEATHERS

DROP OF GLUE

WRAP WITH THREAD

RUN STRING THROUGH

STRING ALL FEATHERS

RUN THROUGH FIRST AGAIN

TIE, THEN GLUE KNOT

FOR SMALL FEATHERS

RUN OUTER TIE-STRING THROUGH IN SAME WAY –

BUSTLE TRICKS

1. If your feathers have too much curve bustle will be cupped like a wash-basin instead of spr ing wide and open. Straighten the feathers by crea the backside of the shaft with a cold chisel or sin instrument at intervals of every half inch.

2. Select feathers for each row that are either rights or all lefts if possible—if mixed they canno spread so evenly.

3. On big feathers, a loop should be made a butt end by cutting the quill at an angle with a sa razor blade and tucking the end up inside, as in the d ing. Always clip off the corners of the loop so that it i wider than the shaft itself—use *manicure scissors* for

4. For small feathers wrap the butt end thread and run the string directly through this wrap end. Save time by putting a drop of airplane glue on end before wrapping, then the thread will not need t tied. String the feathers with a darning needle and o nary string. *Note the method of tying in the drawin*

5. Run the outer tie-string through in the s way, but before tying spread the circle of feathers table, put a circular weight such as a pop bottle in center, and space the feathers equally. Then tighten string and tie. The weight aids greatly in spacing.

THEN

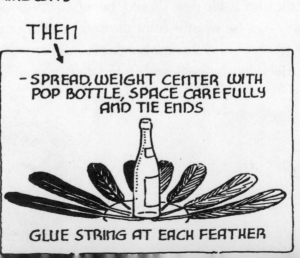

– SPREAD, WEIGHT CENTER WITH POP BOTTLE, SPACE CAREFULLY AND TIE ENDS

GLUE STRING AT EACH FEATHER

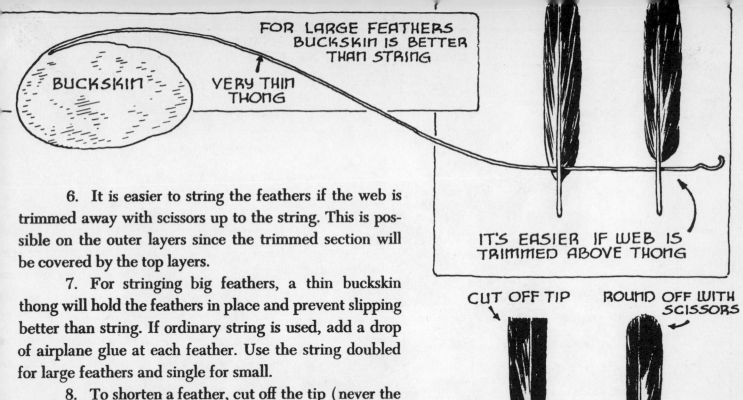

BUCKSKIN

VERY THIN THONG

FOR LARGE FEATHERS BUCKSKIN IS BETTER THAN STRING

IT'S EASIER IF WEB IS TRIMMED ABOVE THONG

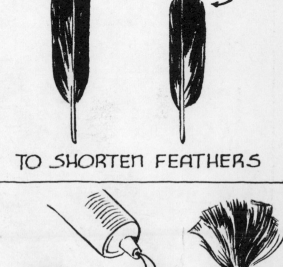

CUT OFF TIP

ROUND OFF WITH SCISSORS

TO SHORTEN FEATHERS

6. It is easier to string the feathers if the web is trimmed away with scissors up to the string. This is possible on the outer layers since the trimmed section will be covered by the top layers.

7. For stringing big feathers, a thin buckskin thong will hold the feathers in place and prevent slipping better than string. If ordinary string is used, add a drop of airplane glue at each feather. Use the string doubled for large feathers and single for small.

8. To shorten a feather, cut off the tip (never the butt end), and round off the web with scissors. A stronger bustle will result if *all* the feathers are shortened in this way, selecting larger ones than needed and clipping off the flimsy tips.

9. A single tip fluffy can be applied with a drop of glue. However, good bustles require a cluster of several fluffies at the tip. To apply these, trim the tip as illustrated and both glue and tie with thread.

10. For the back support, use a No. 10 tin-can top—if smaller than that the bustle may collapse. For large bustles, the cone-shaped rawhide support illustrated is excellent, but not essential. No. 2 can tops are ideal to reinforce the center rosette.

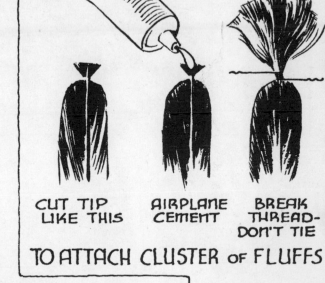

CUT TIP LIKE THIS

AIRPLANE CEMENT

BREAK THREAD— DON'T TIE

TO ATTACH CLUSTER OF FLUFFS

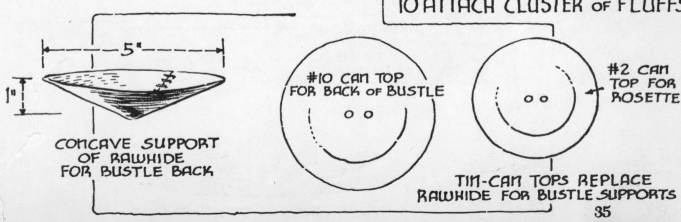

5"

1"

CONCAVE SUPPORT OF RAWHIDE FOR BUSTLE BACK

#10 CAN TOP FOR BACK OF BUSTLE

#2 CAN TOP FOR ROSETTE

TIN-CAN TOPS REPLACE RAWHIDE FOR BUSTLE SUPPORTS

35

OKLAHOMA BUSTLES

THESE GORGEOUS WHEELS of color, characteristic of the tribes of the Oklahoma region, are resplendent beyond compare. They are often worn in sets of four instead of three, a neck bustle being added, as seen on the dancer of the opposite page. So decked out, any dancer becomes a striking figure.

These bustles differ from the Sioux type already described in that fewer layers of feathers are used, and each feather is more carefully tailored and more fully adorned. They vary greatly in detail but the basic construction is always the same. The set here described is that seen on the opposite page; strikingly different effects could be obtained in this same set by changing the color schemes of the fluffies. This chapter describes the standard Oklahoma type; variations of it appear in the pages that follow.

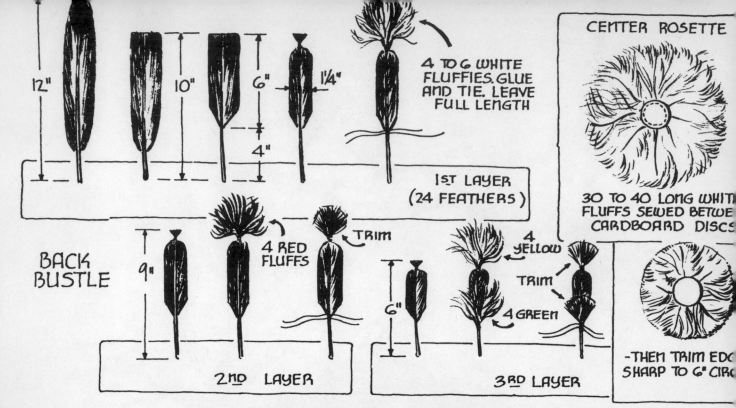

BACK BUSTLE

12"

10"

6"

1¼"

4"

4 TO 6 WHITE FLUFFIES. GLUE AND TIE. LEAVE FULL LENGTH

1ST LAYER (24 FEATHERS)

9"

4 RED FLUFFS

TRIM

2ND LAYER

6"

4 YELLOW

TRIM

4 GREEN

3RD LAYER

CENTER ROSETTE

30 TO 40 LONG WHITE FLUFFS SEWED BETWEEN CARDBOARD DISCS

-THEM TRIM EDGE SHARP TO 6" CIRCLE

ARM BUSTLE

WHITE

1ST LAYER

9"

GREEN TRIMMED

2ND LAYER

6"

RED TRIMMED

4"

YELLOW TRIMMED

3RD LAYER

Three rows of feathers go into each bustle. Use feathers larger than the actual size desired and trim down so as to remove all flimsy parts. The best results are obtained by using dark eagle feathers, but goose pointers, turkey, or other large feathers will serve.

For the back bustle, 24 feathers, 12 or more inches in length, are needed for the outer row. Trim each feather carefully to the size and shape shown in the drawings. Attach six long white fluffies to the tip (see page 35 for method), and leave these fluffies full length. String the feathers as already described. Make the second and third rows in the same way, of the size shown, but *clip the fluffies down*, removing the fuzzy tips and sides to make a neat, trim cluster.

The center rosette is made of many rows of long white fluffies placed on top each other and sewed between two two-inch cardboard discs with a sewing machine—be generous with the fluffs if you would make a good rosette. Using a cardboard disc six inches in diameter as a guide, cut off the ends of the fluffies to a sharp edge, thus making the rosette six inches wide. The convex side of the rosette is the top side. Glue a beaded rosette at the center if possible, otherwise a mirror.

The neck bustle duplicates the back one, with the feathers in each row one inch shorter. The arm bustles are similar except that the feathers in the outer row are trimmed to a point as in the sketch.

The bustles as here described are of average size, the back bustle measuring 28 inches in diameter, and the arm bustles 24 inches. Larger ones are often made, of which those on the dancer at the top of the preceding page are examples, the tail bustle being a full 36 inches, and the arms 30 inches.

These bustles are most effective when worn with a feather roach to match, made as described on page 26.

BUTTERFLIES

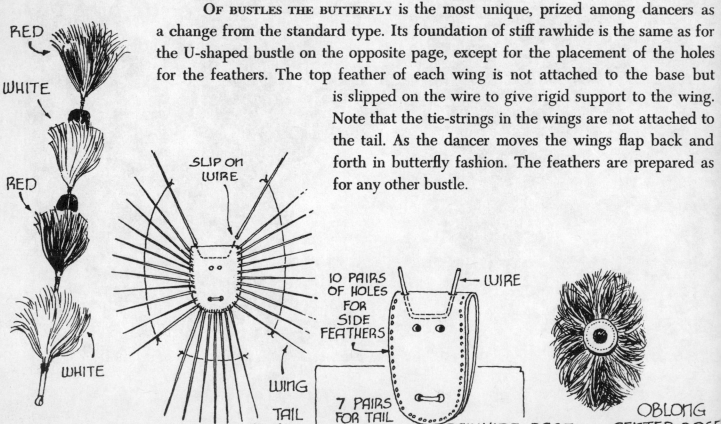

RED

WHITE

RED

WHITE

SLIP ON WIRE

WING

TAIL

10 PAIRS OF HOLES FOR SIDE FEATHERS

WIRE

7 PAIRS FOR TAIL

RAWHIDE BASE

OBLONG CENTER ROSE

Of bustles the butterfly is the most unique, prized among dancers as a change from the standard type. Its foundation of stiff rawhide is the same as for the U-shaped bustle on the opposite page, except for the placement of the holes for the feathers. The top feather of each wing is not attached to the base but is slipped on the wire to give rigid support to the wing. Note that the tie-strings in the wings are not attached to the tail. As the dancer moves the wings flap back and forth in butterfly fashion. The feathers are prepared as for any other bustle.

40

T-SHAPED

BUSTLE

WITH

SPIKES

THIS ENGAGING TYPE OF BUSTLE is styled around two long upright spikes. The foundation is of stiff rawhide—soak until flexible, punch the holes, fold and place under a weight as shown until dry and stiff. Make the wire arrangement of No. 14 wire and insert. Lace the feathers along the edges of the base with a fine buckskin thong. The spikes are made of 18-inch spiked eagle wing feathers and are slipped on the wire. The outer tie-string, preferably a buckskin thong, is run through all feathers including the spikes, and the ends are tied between the spikes with a bow-knot. To collapse, untie this tie-string, slip the spikes off the wire and lay them on top the other feathers.

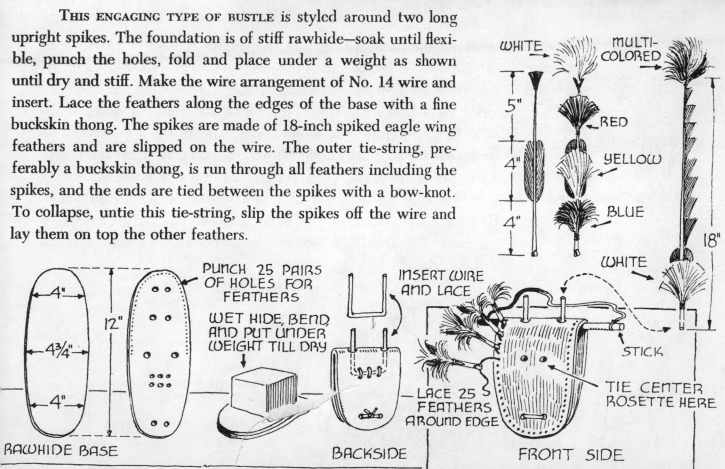

SUNBURSTS

OF ALL BUSTLES, the most brilliant are the sunbursts, their vivid rows of yellow and white bringing a bright splash of sunshine into every setting. For the back bustle, 24 feathers are needed, extra large in size so that when the web is all stripped off a heavy shaft remains. These are then cut down to 10 inches. To them, clusters of white and yellow fluffies are attached in the order shown, six fluffies to the cluster, the end cluster left full length and the others trimmed. Then prepare 24 quills of equal sturdiness four inches long, to the ends of which yellow fluffies are attached. Lay the short circle in the large, and add the center rosette as shown. The arm quills are one inch shorter. The feather roach should match.

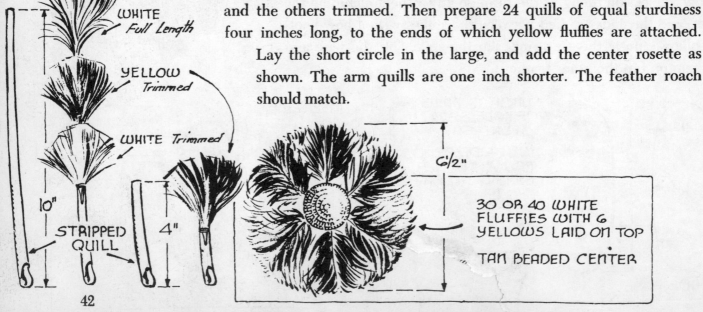

WHITE *Full Length*

YELLOW *Trimmed*

WHITE *Trimmed*

10"

STRIPPED QUILL

4"

6½"

30 OR 40 WHITE FLUFFIES WITH 6 YELLOWS LAID ON TOP

TAN BEADED CENTER

42

CROW

CROW IS A Sioux term meaning *bustle*, but it has come to mean specifically a complete bustle of the ancient type which, in addition to the usual circle of feathers, has two long spikes above, and two pendants of cloth hanging down the legs behind. As illustrated on this page,   the foundation is of stiff rawhide, constructed as described on page 41, with a wire insert on which the spikes are slipped. The spikes are 18-inch eagle wing feathers. The pendants are of blue felt edged with red, long enough to reach almost to the ground, and are covered with 6- to 8-inch white eagle feathers or other attractive feathers of similar size. The bustle proper is usually of dark feathers but any can be used.

BUSTLE STYLES

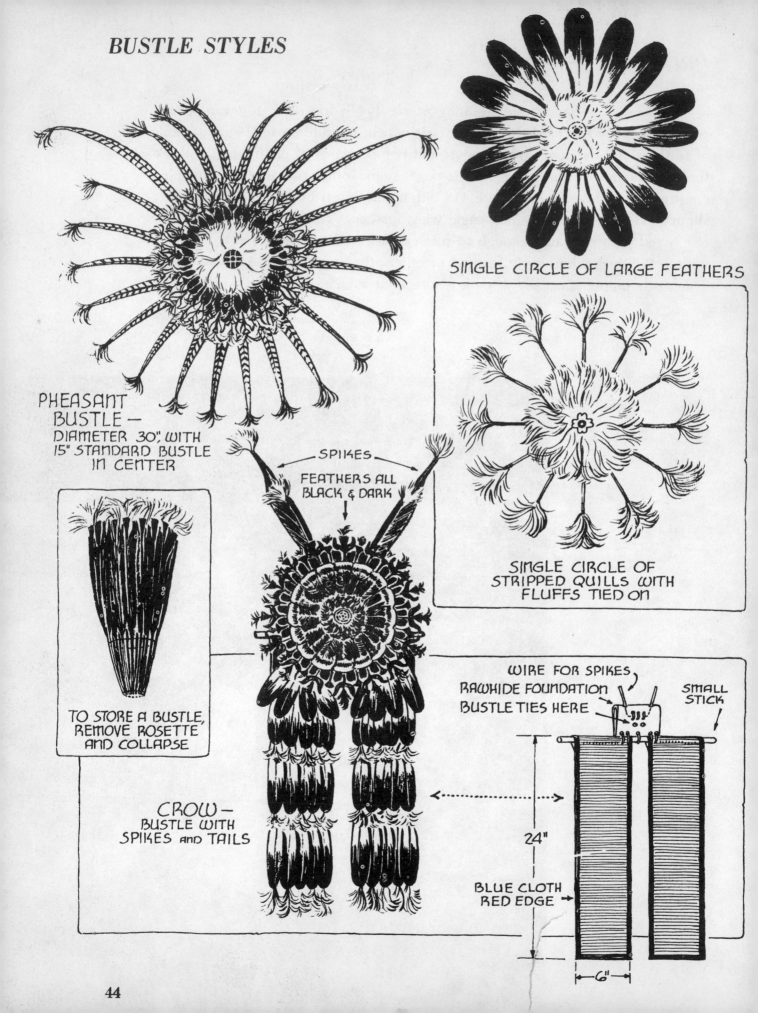

SINGLE CIRCLE OF LARGE FEATHERS

PHEASANT
BUSTLE —
DIAMETER 30", WITH
15" STANDARD BUSTLE
IN CENTER

SPIKES

FEATHERS ALL
BLACK & DARK

SINGLE CIRCLE OF
STRIPPED QUILLS WITH
FLUFFS TIED ON

TO STORE A BUSTLE,
REMOVE ROSETTE
AND COLLAPSE

CROW —
BUSTLE WITH
SPIKES and TAILS

WIRE FOR SPIKES
RAWHIDE FOUNDATION
BUSTLE TIES HERE

SMALL
STICK

24"

BLUE CLOTH
RED EDGE

6"

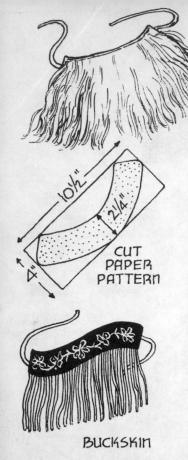

10½"

2¼"

4"

CUT
PAPER
PATTERN

ANGORA   →RED YARN←   5" FR

BUCKSKIN

ANKLETS

ANKLETS ARE WORN JUST above the moccasin and fan out over the foot. They add much sparkle to a dancer's feet. They may be tied either above or below the ankle bells. The one and only material, if to be had, is *angora* with its long, silken, cream-white hair. Make a pattern as shown, cut the angora, and sew it to a backing of canvas.

Of the materials easier to obtain, *yarn* is much used by the Indians nowadays, attached to felt or fur. The felt foundation measures 5 by 11 inches. Cut the yarn into 6-inch lengths, extend it out from the edge, a *thick layer* of it, overlapping the edge one inch. Fold the felt over it and sew—the felt is thus 2½ inches wide and the fringe 5 inches. If of fur, back it with canvas and sew the yarn between. The Woodland tribes often use a strip of beaded cloth with a fringe.

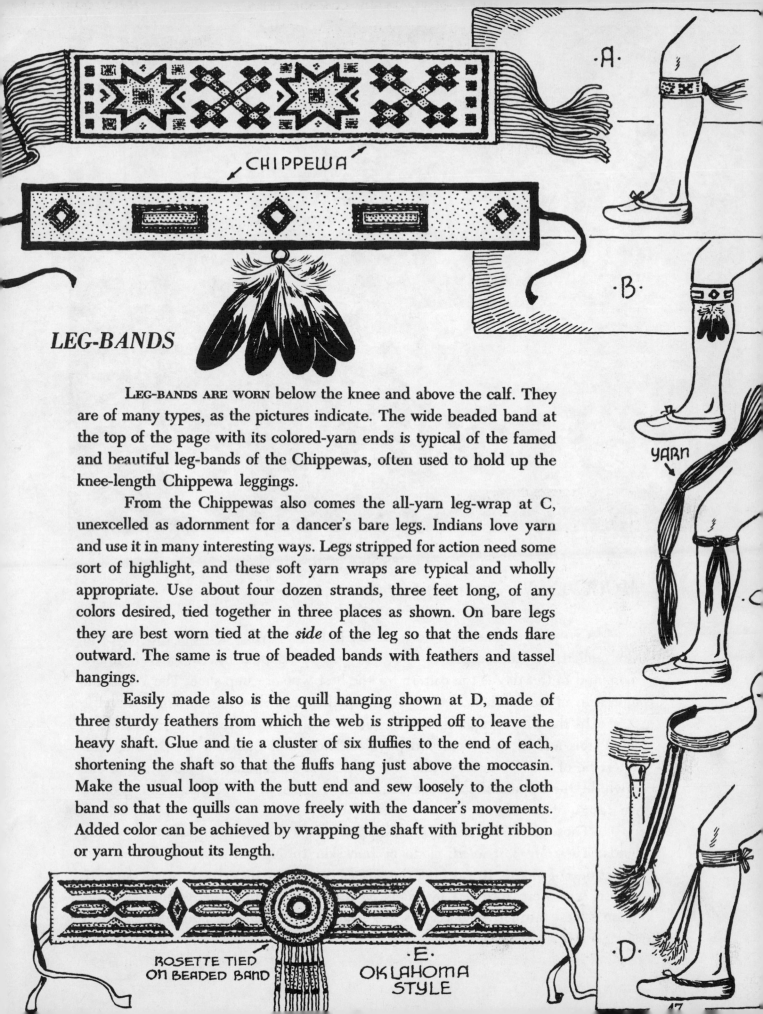

CHIPPEWA

LEG-BANDS

LEG-BANDS ARE WORN below the knee and above the calf. They are of many types, as the pictures indicate. The wide beaded band at the top of the page with its colored-yarn ends is typical of the famed and beautiful leg-bands of the Chippewas, often used to hold up the knee-length Chippewa leggings.

From the Chippewas also comes the all-yarn leg-wrap at C, unexcelled as adornment for a dancer's bare legs. Indians love yarn and use it in many interesting ways. Legs stripped for action need some sort of highlight, and these soft yarn wraps are typical and wholly appropriate. Use about four dozen strands, three feet long, of any colors desired, tied together in three places as shown. On bare legs they are best worn tied at the *side* of the leg so that the ends flare outward. The same is true of beaded bands with feathers and tassel hangings.

Easily made also is the quill hanging shown at D, made of three sturdy feathers from which the web is stripped off to leave the heavy shaft. Glue and tie a cluster of six fluffies to the end of each, shortening the shaft so that the fluffs hang just above the moccasin. Make the usual loop with the butt end and sew loosely to the cloth band so that the quills can move freely with the dancer's movements. Added color can be achieved by wrapping the shaft with bright ribbon or yarn throughout its length.

·A.

·B.

YARN

·C·

·D·

ROSETTE TIED
ON BEADED BAND

·E·
OKLAHOMA
STYLE

47

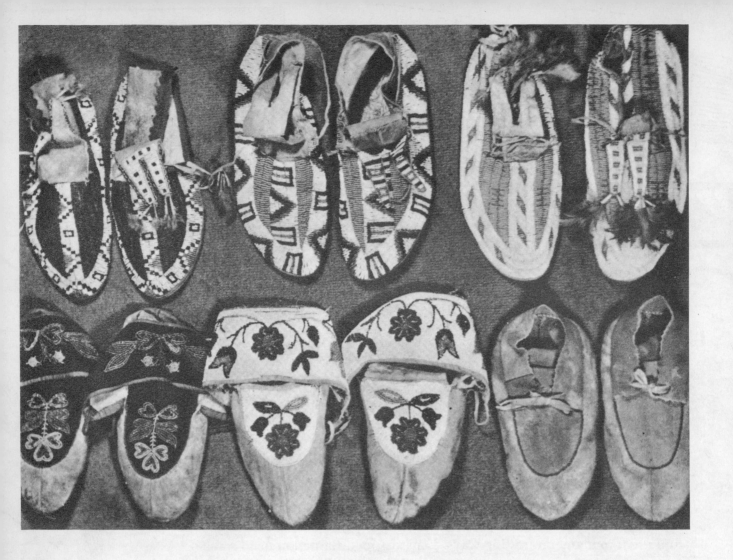

MOCCASINS

ONE OF THE GREATEST GIFTS of the Indian to civilization was the moccasin. Unexcelled for wilderness travel, it was quickly adopted by the early frontiersmen, and to this day is the pattern for the best type of camp shoe. The Woodland moccasin of buckskin has never been equalled as a shoe for snowshoe travel.

In the photograph above, we see the contrast between the moccasins of the Plains and of the Woodland peoples. Those in the top row are Dakota, characteristic of the Plains type—they are *hard-soled* moccasins. The soles are of stiff rawhide, the uppers of soft buckskin, solidly beaded in the characteristic geometric design of the Plains.

Those in the lower row are Chippewa, typical of the footgear of the Woodlands. They are *soft-soled,* made of buckskin throughout, usually of deer but sometimes of moose. It was from the wearing of such as these by the early pioneers, whose feet were softened by many years in shoes, that the word *tenderfoot* arose. These attractive moccasins are beaded in the familiar *floral* design of the

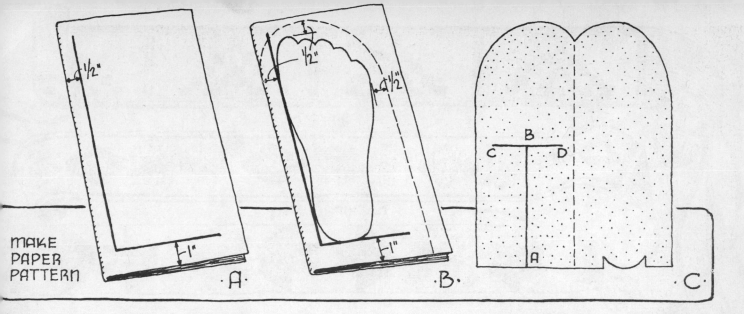

MAKE PAPER PATTERN

·A·   ·B·   ·C·

·D·

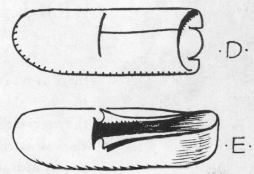

·E·

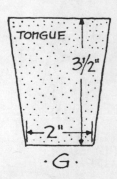

·F·

Woodland folk. Sometimes the tongue piece and the ankle strip are solidly beaded, sometimes only partially, and indeed on everyday or "work" moccasins, not at all. A characteristic treatment in decoration is to make the upper parts of black or blue cloth to match the beaded clothing worn.

In the Southwest desert region, a still different type of moccasin is used, of angle height; but, not being particularly attractive, it has never become popular outside that area.

Moccasins of the types in the photograph are not easy to make. The Plains Indian, however, also used on occasion a *soft-soled* type which happily is easily constructed. By following the simple pattern in the drawings an excellent serviceable moccasin can be produced.

Use any soft leather such as calf or sheep, and sew with heavy linen thread. First make a paper pattern as shown at A and B, placing the full weight on the foot in making the tracing, and holding the pencil straight up and down. Spread the pattern as in C, draw the lines A-B and C-D and cut along them. Now try the pattern on the foot for size and adjust it as necessary—feet vary in size and shape so much that there is no way to secure a moccasin that fits except by experimenting with a pattern.

Cut the leather, turn it wrong side out, and sew along the side as in D—moccasins are always sewn wrong side out and then reversed. Before sewing up the back as in F, check for size again. The tongue is then cut to fit and sewed on.

In another book, *Woodcraft*, I have described how the hard-soled Plains moccasins and the Woodland moccasins are made.

TONGUE   3½"   2"

·G·

·H·

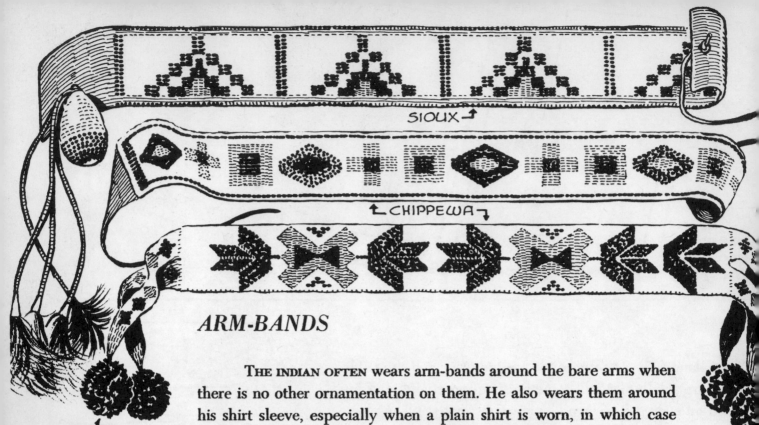

SIOUX →

← CHIPPEWA →

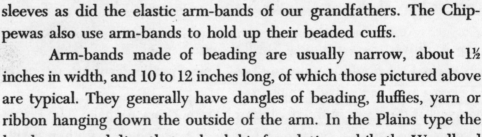

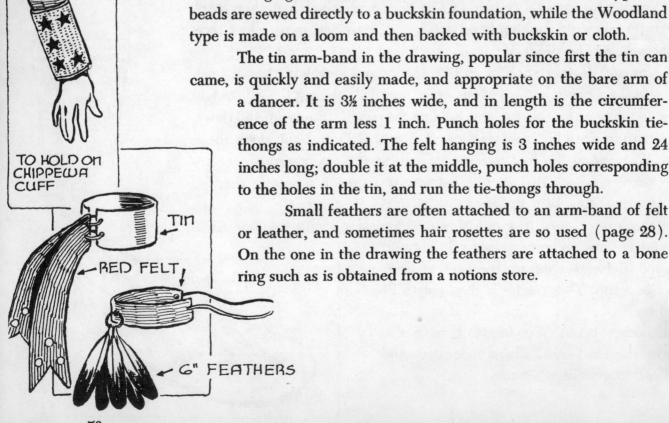

POMPONS
OF YARN

TO HOLD ON
CHIPPEWA
CUFF

TIN

← RED FELT →

← 6" FEATHERS

ARM-BANDS

THE INDIAN OFTEN wears arm-bands around the bare arms when there is no other ornamentation on them. He also wears them around his shirt sleeve, especially when a plain shirt is worn, in which case they serve the dual purpose of decoration and utility, holding up the sleeves as did the elastic arm-bands of our grandfathers. The Chippewas also use arm-bands to hold up their beaded cuffs.

Arm-bands made of beading are usually narrow, about 1½ inches in width, and 10 to 12 inches long, of which those pictured above are typical. They generally have dangles of beading, fluffies, yarn or ribbon hanging down the outside of the arm. In the Plains type the beads are sewed directly to a buckskin foundation, while the Woodland type is made on a loom and then backed with buckskin or cloth.

The tin arm-band in the drawing, popular since first the tin can came, is quickly and easily made, and appropriate on the bare arm of a dancer. It is 3½ inches wide, and in length is the circumference of the arm less 1 inch. Punch holes for the buckskin tie-thongs as indicated. The felt hanging is 3 inches wide and 24 inches long; double it at the middle, punch holes corresponding to the holes in the tin, and run the tie-thongs through.

Small feathers are often attached to an arm-band of felt or leather, and sometimes hair rosettes are so used (page 28). On the one in the drawing the feathers are attached to a bone ring such as is obtained from a notions store.

DANCER'S BREECHCLOTHS

ACTIVE DANCERS USUALLY prefer body paint to clothing and wear a breech-cloth only. Under such conditions, the breechcloth should be inconspicuous, fading into the background and attracting no attention to itself. It should be of soft, attractive material, such as flannel, fine corduroy or velvet. Overlarge and bulky breech-cloths attract attention undesirably. Nine inches is the proper width; the length depends on the wearer. It is worn slightly longer in back than in front. The standard type is one long strip as in A; when fine cloth is used, a middle section of calico as in B reduces the cost. These are held with a separate tie-string. The breechcloth at C has front and back aprons with a tie-string passing through. The breechcloth should be of a solid color, unadorned except possibly for a half-inch edge of a contrasting color.

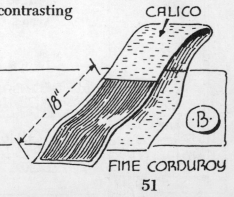

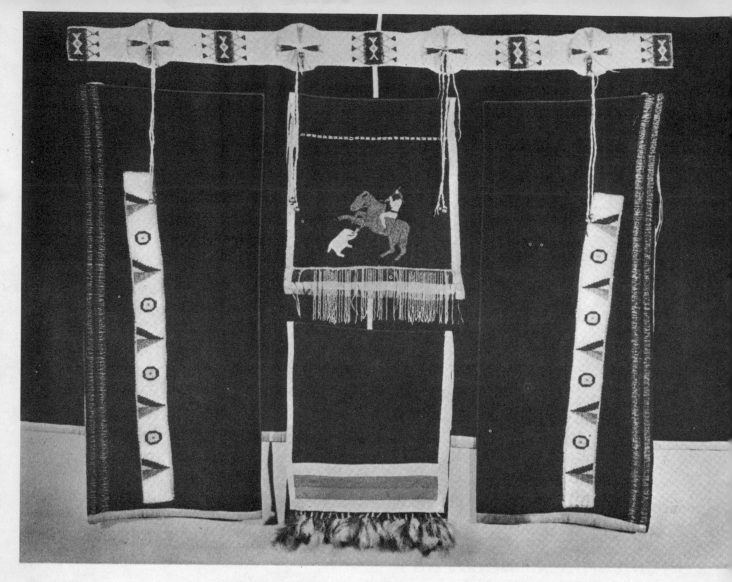

PLAINS LEGGINGS AND BREECHCLOTHS

LEGGINGS WERE FIRST MADE OF buckskin and later of the famous government-issued wool "list cloth"—the Dakota leggings in the photograph are of this cloth; the fancy woven-in edge labels it. Nowadays any good heavy wool cloth is used. The standard color is dark blue. Cut 28 inches wide, fold, and sew at the angle shown in the drawing, thus leaving a wide flap. The length depends on the wearer. Edge with yellow. The beaded strip goes on the legging proper, not the flap.

The breechcloth should match in color and material. It is 13 inches wide, the length depending on the wearer. Beading on breechcloth is less typical than the series of colored stripes across the bottom—red, yellow, white and light blue.

The Plains list-cloth blanket in the photograph, 56 by 96 inches, shows the famed beaded shoulder rosette strip, 3 inches wide by 4 feet.

TIES TO BELT

2"

3"

BEADED BAND—
2½" WIDE, 26" LONG

4½"

14"

LEGGINGS—
EITHER SOFT LEATHER
OR WOOL CLOTH

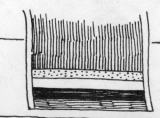

BREECHCLOTH—
3 OR 4 COLORED CLOTH
STRIPES, ¾", ACROSS BOTTOM
NO BEADING.

WOODLAND LEGGINGS AND APRONS

THE CONTRAST BETWEEN the decorative design and the clothing of the Woodland and Plains tribes is clearly apparent by comparing the Chippewa garments in floral design on this page with those of the Dakota styled in geometric pattern on the opposite page.

The favorite cloth of the northern Woodlands is *velvet,* either dark blue or deep maroon. Bright colors are rarely seen, and the beading, too, although generous in quantity, avoids all suggestion of overcoloring and gaudiness.

The leggings are nearly straight, with no flap, measuring about 9 inches at the bottom and 11 at the top; they extend to the crotch and are tied to the belt with two thongs. The beading extends up the front side only, except on the cuff where it is carried all the way around. Another type of legging, shown in the bottom corners, extends only to the knees and is slipped on over a pair of ordinary trousers, held in place by a beaded leg-band.

The Chippewas do not wear breechcloths in the usual sense, but instead use the gorgeous *aprons* for which they are noted, a fine example of which appears in the middle of the photograph. The aprons are square, 18 to 20 inches more or less, depending on the wearer. Two are worn, front and back, and tied around the waist.

In all these garments the beading is sewed directly to the cloth, but in the case of velvet, it is backed with other material to give it sufficient body, the bead threads going through both materials.

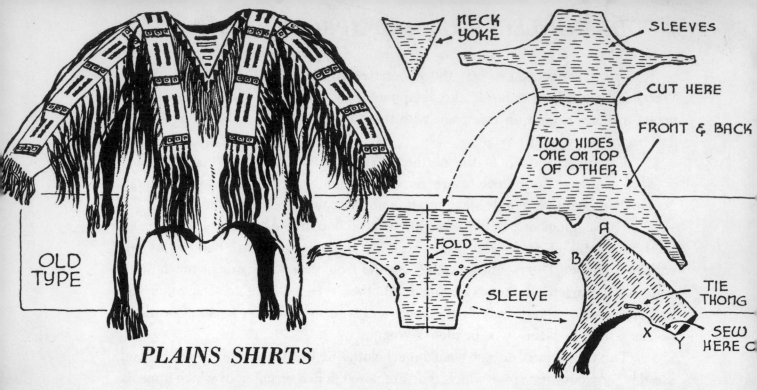

PLAINS SHIRTS

TWO SOFT-TANNED HIDES are placed one on top the other, and cut as shown in the pattern above. The front-leg sections make the arms, and the large pieces the front and back. Trim the hide for the neck and shoulders along the dotted lines, making the neck hole just large enough to slip the head through. First sew the triangular yokes to the neck, front and back, and let them hang loose. With the hides inside out, sew together at the shoulders. Then shape the sleeves as shown and sew the end AB to the shirt. The sides of the shirt are held together with tie-thongs (not sewed) at intervals of six inches. The neck should be finished with an inch-wide hem of red cloth or buckskin.

The new-style shirt differs in that the long leg sections are trimmed off, and the shirt more carefully tailored. Use your own shirt for size, enlarging it a good inch. The shirt may be sewed throughout if preferred.

The beaded bands are made separately and sewed on. Imitations can be made with paint on muslin. The locks of hair were not scalp-locks, but were usually donated by relatives and friends. Use wig hair, switches, or even black horsehair. Attach by needling the thong through the hide and tying a knot on the inside of the shirt.

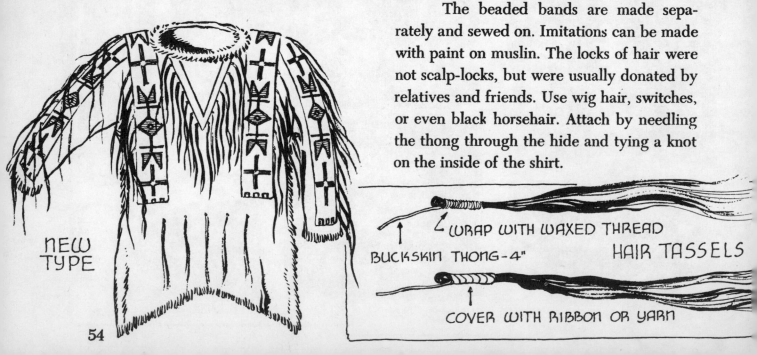

WOODLAND

MODERN

UCKSKIN SHIRTS

THESE ARE THE SHIRTS of the Woodland Redmen, the true buckskin shirts of :erhide. In the old days they were made much as on the Plains, but much earlier an on the Plains, were tailored more carefully in the shoulders and sleeves, and wed instead of laced. Of these, the Woodland shirt shown above is typical. As :ual in buckskin sewing, this shirt was sewed inside-out and then reversed. To rm the shoulder fringes, two extra pieces of hide are sewed in the shoulder seam, oubled down front and back and sewed again about two or three inches from the oulder seam as shown. Below this the hide is fringed. An extra piece is also sewed the seams between the shoulder and sleeve for the fringe.

Still more recently the Woods Indians copied our modern tailored shirts but ten beaded the shoulders in floral design as in the drawing. The beading is ap-ied to a second piece of buckskin, thus aking a double shoulder. Indeed, shirts ordinary black cotton cloth were often eaded across the shoulder in this way.

The Hopi shirt is characterized by e way the seams are sewed: It is sewed ght-side out, the excess hide trimmed off ie inch from the seam, and this inch-wide maining edge then fringed. The fringes us stand straight up.

TWIG

RAWHIDE

TIE KNOT ON INSIDE OF SHIRT

WOOD BUTTONS

HOW HOPI SEAMS ARE SEWED

SOUTHWEST (HOPI)

PLAINS VESTS AND CUFFS

OVER A BEADED WAR-SHIRT no other ornamentation is needed or often used, save perhaps necklaces, for the shirt is beautiful enough in itself—too beautiful to cover. It is when a plain shirt is worn that the fancy vest, or the breastplates described in the next two pages, are sought.

In making a vest, use your own vest as a pattern, enlarging it by an inch since the vest should fit loosely. Cut the bottom square and shape it in general as in the drawing. Buckskin or any soft-tanned leather in natural color may be used.

Vests are usually beaded solidly front and back, with the background around the design typically in solid white. Some vests are but partially beaded, with the leather itself used as the background. The designs are of two types, either *geometric* as at the top of the page, or *natural,* showing a realistic picture

CUFFS

such as a horse or buffalo. Among the old-time Sioux, this depended on who did the beading, whether women or men, the women always doing geometric and the men natural designs. The geometric designs are usually considered more appropriate and are preferred. And they are easier to do, in that the simple lazy stitch is used, the how of it described on page 106.

Vests are worn with beaded cuffs and arm-bands. Shape the cuff as in the drawing, making a paper pattern for fit. Its length is six inches. Arm-bands have already been described. All three items should hang together in color and type of design.

BONE BEAD - 4½" TO 5½" LONG

HAIR-PIPE BREASTPLATES

THROUGHOUT A LONG yesterday these striking breastplates adorned the proud lords of the Western Plains and their women, made from long slender bone "beads" called *hair-pipes*. The pipes are about ¼-inch thick at the middle and taper toward the end, and vary from 3½ to 5½ inches long. The longer ones are hung in two rows, the shorter in three rows.

Of the present-day materials easily obtained, the best imitation is the stem of a corncob pipe bought inexpensively from a cigar store. About 90 are needed. They should be carefully coated with ivory enamel to imitate bone, best done by stringing them on a long cord or wire. Needed also are about 200 large beads of the thickness of the pipe at the widest part, either of wood, brass, or glass, of any color desired. •Four straps of thick harness leather ⅜ inches wide and 15 inches long, and a quantity of buckskin thongs complete the equipment.

Punch holes in the leather straps at regular intervals, so spaced that the pipes will almost touch each other. Tie a knot in a buckskin thong, leaving a 1½ inch end, and string through the straps, pipes, and beads in the order shown. Stretch tight and tie a similar knot at the opposite end. Three or four beads go in the center in any combination of colors desired.

The completed breastplate should be about 12 inches wide and 12 to 15 inches long, reaching to the waist when worn. The V-shaped tie-strings at the top extend to the side of the neck.

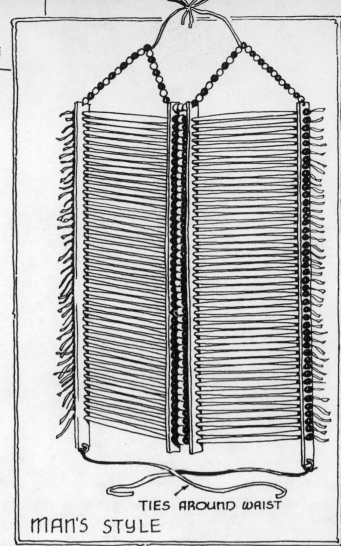

TIES AROUND WAIST

MAN'S STYLE

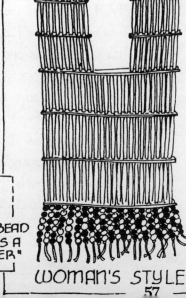

WOMAN'S STYLE

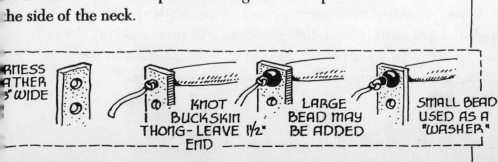

RNESS ATHER ⅜" WIDE

KNOT BUCKSKIN THONG - LEAVE 1½" END

LARGE BEAD MAY BE ADDED

SMALL BEAD USED AS A "WASHER"

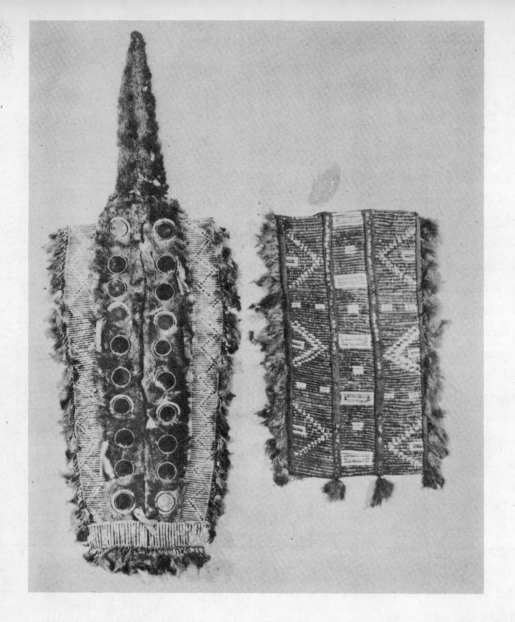

QUILL BREASTPLATES AND OTTERS

THESE ARE THE RARE old breastplates of the quill-work that was the fore-runner of beading, much loved on the western prairies. Porcupine quills were dyed, then flattened and wrapped around ¼-inch strips of rawhide, which in turn were sewed horizontally to a buckskin foundation so as to create the design. The background is red with the figures in green, yellow and white.

The rectangular type to the right, measuring 12 by 24 inches, is edged with red fluffies held in tiny tin cones (page 69). More highly regarded is the famed *otter* type at the left, the otter skin being the most valued of all hides. The hide is split as shown, decorated with mirrors, and edged with quill-work. The head goes through the split, with a neck-thong holding it at proper height, the tail extending down the back. To wear one of these otter breastplates is to wear one of the good and dignified garments worthy of a man of importance.

PLAINS CLOTHING (SIOUX)

WOODLAND VESTS

ALMOST INVARIABLY they are made of velvet, either black, dark blue, or deep maroon, and heavily beaded in floral design. They consist of two panels attached at the shoulders, with an opening for the head, and hang down over the chest and back, the weight of the beading keeping them in place. One shoulder is sewed together and the other equipped with buttons. They are worn with cuffs to match. The pattern for the vest at the right is shown in the drawing. From it, the other styles can be worked out. The velvet is backed with cotton material and the beading applied directly to the velvet.

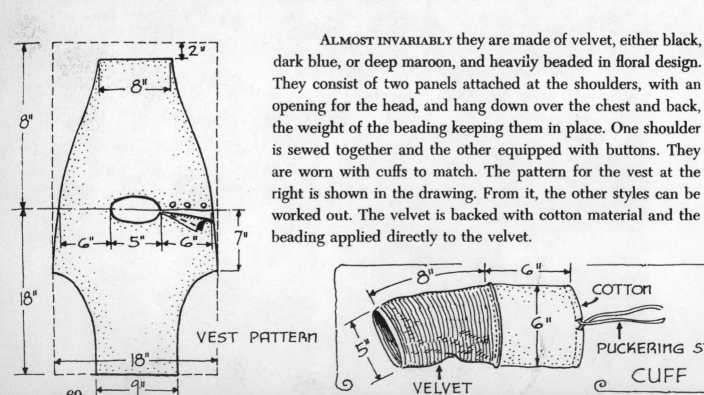

VEST PATTERN

CUFF

60

WOODLAND CLOTHING (CHIPPEWA)

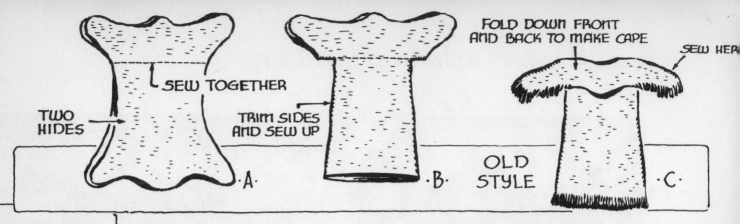

TWO HIDES → SEW TOGETHER ·A·

TRIM SIDES AND SEW UP ·B·

FOLD DOWN FRONT AND BACK TO MAKE CAPE

SEW HER

OLD STYLE ·C·

WOMEN'S LEGGINGS

PLAINS DRESSES AND LEGGINGS

THE DRESSES OF THE WOMEN with their gorgeous yokes of solid beading, often adding 15 pounds to the weight of the dress, were beyond doubt the most beautiful items of clothing on the Plains. The construction is simple enough: Two hides large enough to allow the dress to hang to the knees were placed together *tail ends up*, and sewed together as in A, leaving a hole for the head so that the dress can be slipped on poncho-style. The sides were then trimmed to fit as in B and sewed or laced up. The two flaps above the shoulders were then folded down to form a cape-like yoke as in C, and sewed together at the top edge only. In more recent years the yokes were often made separately and sewed on at the shoulders. A separate belt was used.

The yoke was usually beaded solidly in geometric design, of which those in the pictures are typical. The sleeve ends and the skirt bottom were fringed. Long thongs were often added to the skirt as shown, slipped through two holes so that the ends hung evenly.

The women wore leggings in winter or when in ceremonial dress, covering the leg up to the knees, held by a garter string.

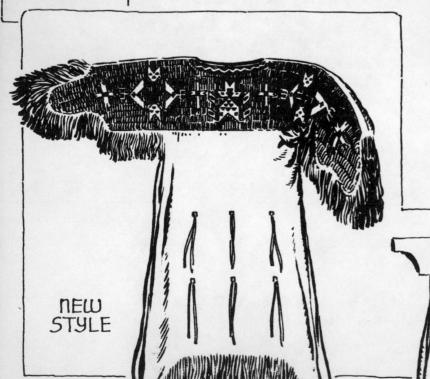

NEW STYLE

CAPE-LIKE YOKE MADE SEPARATE AND ADDED SEWED TO DRESS ACRO SHOULDERS

63

CHIPPEWA DANCE DRESS

RESPLENDENT with fringe upon fringe of tin-cone jingles, the Chippewa woman's dance dress is at once colorful in ap-

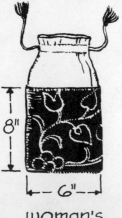

8"

6"

WOMAN'S BAG

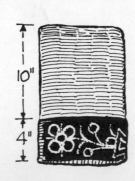

10"

4"

WOMEN'S LEGGINGS

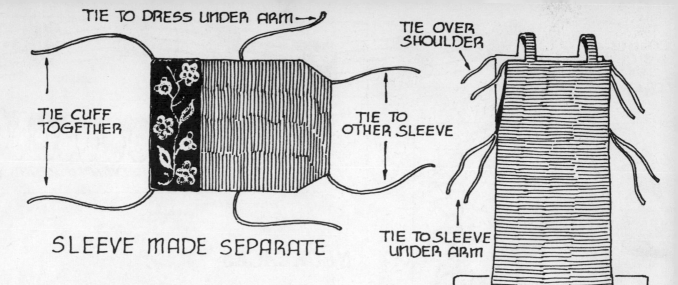

TIE TO DRESS UNDER ARM →

TIE CUFF TOGETHER

TIE TO OTHER SLEEVE

SLEEVE MADE SEPARATE

TIE OVER SHOULDER

TIE TO SLEEVE UNDER ARM

OLD-STYLE DRESS

pearance and vibrant with sound. Made from the lowly tin can, the cones nevertheless have a peculiarly decorative quality. Their weight causes them to swish emphatically with each dancing step, joining the rhythm of the men's bells with their own characteristic metallic rattling sound. It seems to be the sound, more than the decoration, that is sought in these jingle dresses. Thimbles are also often seen on these dresses, used as fringes in this same way.

It is a simple straight dress with 8-inch sleeves, reaching below the knees, made of black velvet to match the dark dancing clothes of the men. There are 100 cones to a fringe, over 700 in all, each two inches long except those on the neck fringe which are one inch. Round spangles of tin about the size of a quarter also add their appeal.

Beaded leggings cover the lower leg and are tied with garter strings just below the knee. The beading is confined to the cuff of velvet matching the dress, and the uppers are of black cotton cloth.

It goes without saying that this type of dress is modern. In ancient days the Woodland dresses were made of hides, sometimes in two pieces—a skirt worn with a man-like shirt, and sometimes a one-piece breast-high dress with sleeves made separately and tied on. It is this latter type that survived into the days of cloth and is still occasionally seen on the old women. As shown in the sketches, the dress is held by shoulder straps, the sleeves tied to it under the arms, and tied to each other in front and in back of the neck. The sleeves have beaded cuffs and there is usually beading on the chest to match. It was because of their lack of sound that beads have given way to jingles on the dance dresses. With this change also came the sewed sleeves and the more modern lines seen in the photograph.

The woman's hat, drawn from samples in the author's possession, is reminiscent of the men's turbans on page 19, except for the long tail and the jingles. As always, the first choice is beaver fur.

WOMAN'S HAT — OF BEAVER FUR WITH TIN JINGLES

ELK'S TEETH - *THE REDMAN'S PEARL* (PLAINS)

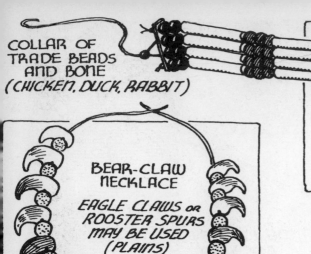

COLLAR OF TRADE BEADS AND BONE (CHICKEN, DUCK, RABBIT)

BEAR-CLAW NECKLACE

EAGLE CLAWS OR ROOSTER SPURS MAY BE USED (PLAINS)

NECKLACES

THEY ARE UNIVERSAL and of many types, adorning the chests of men and women alike. Trade or "store" beads of glass, wood, or brass, strung either in white-man style or interspersed with bits of bone, are common. Chicken, duck, and rabbit bones from the kitchen scraps are suitable, sawed to length, the marrow cleaned out by boiling, then scraped and polished with linseed oil. All the necklace types in the sketches can be easily reproduced, except, of course, the precious elk's teeth which are the most valued of jewels, the Redman's pearls, mark of wealth and importance. The shell concha, always dignified and distinctive as a neck ornament, can be made from a large shell, the rough back filed off down to the white.

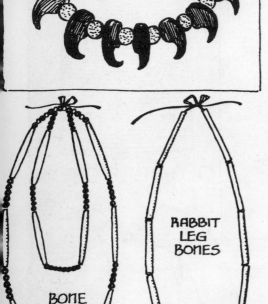

RABBIT LEG BONES

BONE AND BEAD

(CHIPPEWA)

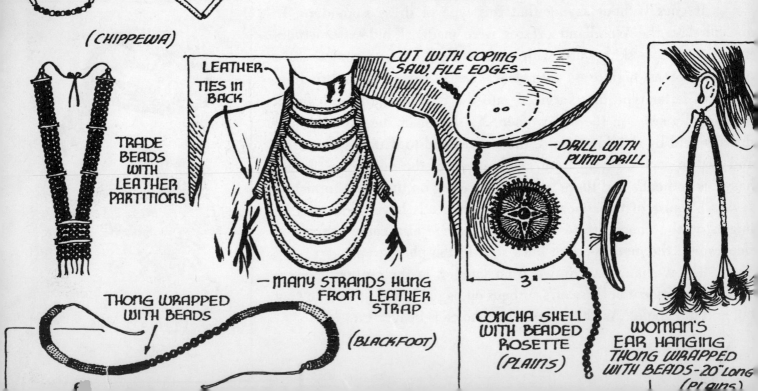

TRADE BEADS WITH LEATHER PARTITIONS

LEATHER TIES IN BACK

CUT WITH COPING SAW, FILE EDGES

—DRILL WITH PUMP DRILL

THONG WRAPPED WITH BEADS

—MANY STRANDS HUNG FROM LEATHER STRAP

(BLACKFOOT)

3"

CONCHA SHELL WITH BEADED ROSETTE (PLAINS)

WOMAN'S EAR HANGING THONG WRAPPED WITH BEADS-20" LONG (PLAINS)

DEWCLAW NECKLACE

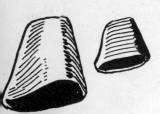

SHEEP TOES

SECTIONS OF
HOOF CARVED

DEW-CLAWS

NOISE-MAKERS THERE MUST BE, attached to the dancer's legs, or as fringes on clothing, or carried in hand, to add the rhythm of sound to that of motion. The ancient type were the famed *dew-claws* of the Plains, the forerunner of the sleighbells so popular in recent years. Jet black and shiny, they make appealing ornaments, but their chief function is sound, for they possess a delightful ringing-rattling quality when shaken against each other.

Pictured above is a section of a 6½-foot necklace in the author's possession, typical of the old Plains type, made of 133 dew-claws attached to a half-inch leather strap, which is slung over one shoulder or doubled around the neck. Dew-claws are made of hoofs. To make them is to fashion an ancient and rare Indian article, of which one can well be proud. Sheep toes are the best source, boiled until they slip off the bone, and held by a thong through a hole drilled in the end. The flat types pictured are of hoofs boiled and separated into layers, then carved and incised with a knife while still soft. Polish with a half-round file and sandpaper, then with a cloth and linseed oil.

As a substitute, chicken bones, cartridge shells, or tin jingles may be used.

CHICKEN BONES

EMPTY CARTRIDGE SHELLS

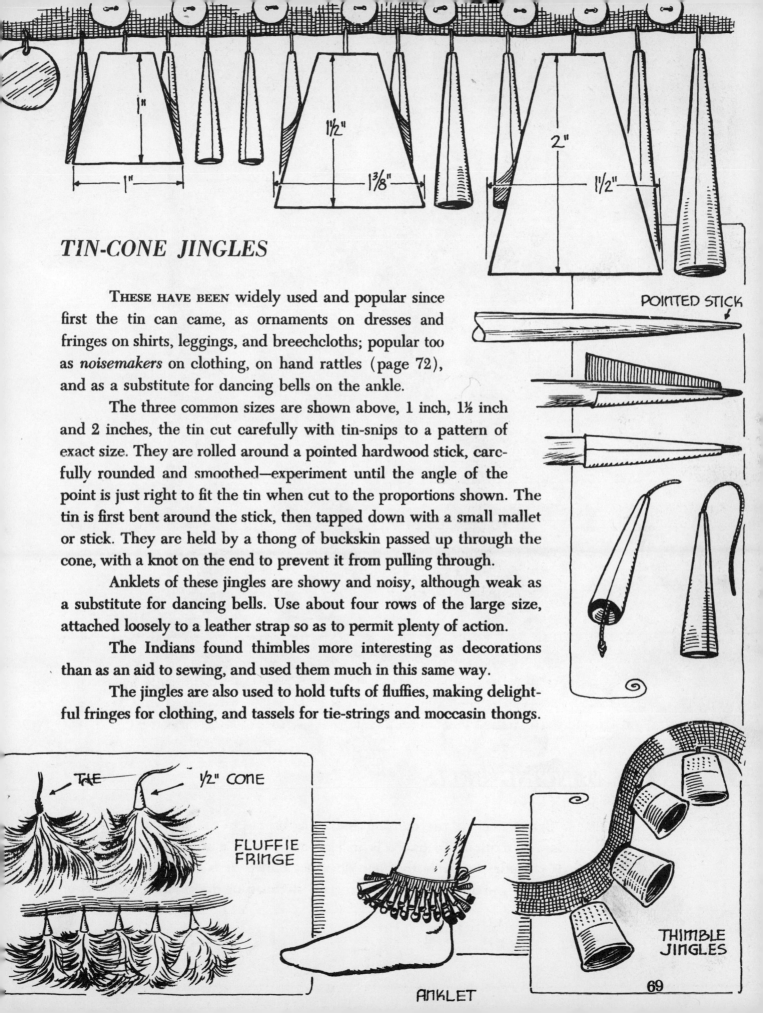

TIN-CONE JINGLES

THESE HAVE BEEN widely used and popular since first the tin can came, as ornaments on dresses and fringes on shirts, leggings, and breechcloths; popular too as *noisemakers* on clothing, on hand rattles (page 72), and as a substitute for dancing bells on the ankle.

The three common sizes are shown above, 1 inch, 1½ inch and 2 inches, the tin cut carefully with tin-snips to a pattern of exact size. They are rolled around a pointed hardwood stick, carefully rounded and smoothed—experiment until the angle of the point is just right to fit the tin when cut to the proportions shown. The tin is first bent around the stick, then tapped down with a small mallet or stick. They are held by a thong of buckskin passed up through the cone, with a knot on the end to prevent it from pulling through.

Anklets of these jingles are showy and noisy, although weak as a substitute for dancing bells. Use about four rows of the large size, attached loosely to a leather strap so as to permit plenty of action.

The Indians found thimbles more interesting as decorations than as an aid to sewing, and used them much in this same way.

The jingles are also used to hold tufts of fluffies, making delightful fringes for clothing, and tassels for tie-strings and moccasin thongs.

POINTED STICK

TIE   ½" CONE

FLUFFIE FRINGE

ANKLET

THIMBLE JINGLES

69

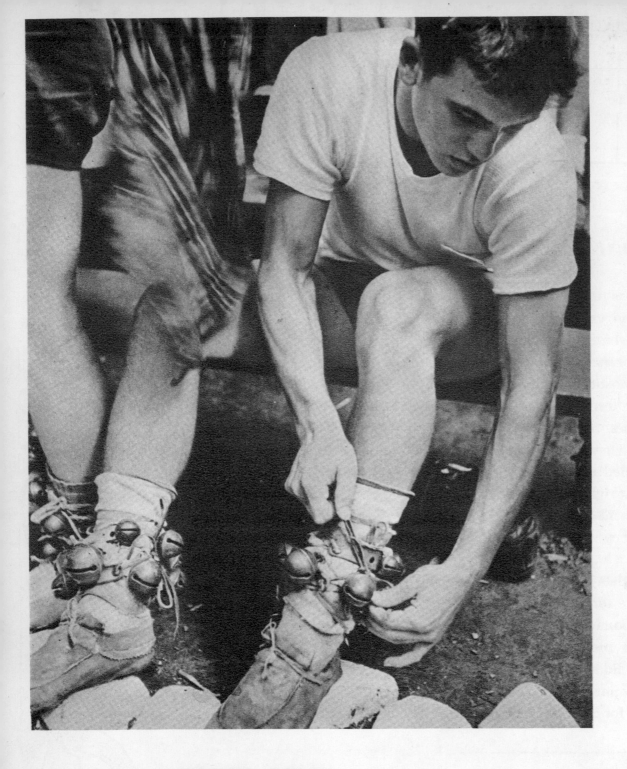

DANCING BELLS

BELLS ARE TO THE dancing Indian as breeze to the sailboat; they are the
medicine of motion. To dance is to ring one's bells, and so, when there are no
bells, it is understandable that one does not dance. It is the same with all who
dance in the Indian way, whether ancient Redman or his modern imitator—once

WAIST BELLS

5 6 7 8 9 10 10 9 8 7 6 5

SHEEP'S WOOL

having worn bells, all effort to dance without them seems futile. The ringing of many bells to the booming drum stirs the soul of all, both dancers and spectators. Other trappings may be mere adornment, but bells are the power to move, indispensable and wholly necessary.

No modern fashion this, for metal bells were worn in Mexico long before the coming of the white man. North of the Rio Grande various types of rattles on the legs were used instead, which quickly and naturally gave way to bells once the trader supplied them.

Good *brass sleighbells* with a loud, clear, musical ring should be diligently sought after—old ones can often be found in secondhand and antique stores. There is no substitute for these—the tiny tin bells sold in dime stores and toy shops are wholly inadequate and useless. This type of bell with a flange held to the strap by wire is the only serviceable one in the rough usage that dance bells receive. The riveted type soon comes off, and once off, cannot be replaced.

The ankle bells are the essential ones, strung 8 to a string. For a light string, use the No. 3 or No. 4 size. Heavier strings may have graduated sizes, from No. 6's down to No. 3's. Strong dancers usually wear two strings, a lighter and a heavier, one above the other. Many Indians prefer bells with a slightly different tone for each ankle.

In addition, a string of bells should be worn around the waist. Here, heavier loud-ringing bells can be carried comfortably and will do much to make the dance heard. There should be about 12 to the string, graduated from No. 10's down to No. 5's. The open type of sleighbell is also excellent for the waist. All bells should harmonize.

Sometimes bells are worn just below the knee, and occasionally a string is run down the outside of the leg from the waist to the knee, but these are not recommended.

Protection for the skin is always needed. Particularly essential are the ankle protectors, made as shown from sheep's wool or scrap saddle felt. For waist bells, a strip should be tied directly to the strap as shown.

THIS TYPE

WIRE

NOT THIS

RIVET

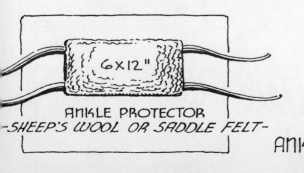

6 X 12"

ANKLE PROTECTOR
-SHEEP'S WOOL OR SADDLE FELT-

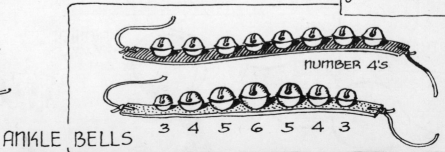

NUMBER 4'S

ANKLE BELLS   3 4 5 6 5 4 3

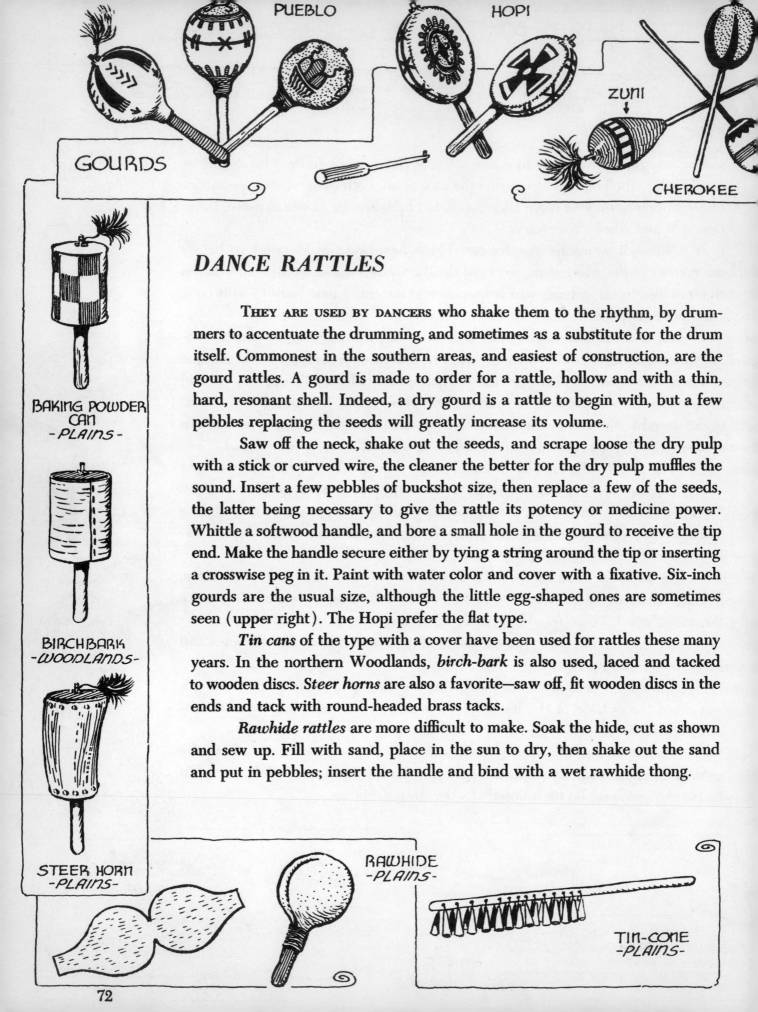

PUEBLO

HOPI

ZUNI

CHEROKEE

GOURDS

BAKING POWDER CAN
-PLAINS-

BIRCHBARK
-WOODLANDS-

STEER HORN
-PLAINS-

DANCE RATTLES

THEY ARE USED BY DANCERS who shake them to the rhythm, by drummers to accentuate the drumming, and sometimes as a substitute for the drum itself. Commonest in the southern areas, and easiest of construction, are the gourd rattles. A gourd is made to order for a rattle, hollow and with a thin, hard, resonant shell. Indeed, a dry gourd is a rattle to begin with, but a few pebbles replacing the seeds will greatly increase its volume.

Saw off the neck, shake out the seeds, and scrape loose the dry pulp with a stick or curved wire, the cleaner the better for the dry pulp muffles the sound. Insert a few pebbles of buckshot size, then replace a few of the seeds, the latter being necessary to give the rattle its potency or medicine power. Whittle a softwood handle, and bore a small hole in the gourd to receive the tip end. Make the handle secure either by tying a string around the tip or inserting a crosswise peg in it. Paint with water color and cover with a fixative. Six-inch gourds are the usual size, although the little egg-shaped ones are sometimes seen (upper right). The Hopi prefer the flat type.

Tin cans of the type with a cover have been used for rattles these many years. In the northern Woodlands, *birch-bark* is also used, laced and tacked to wooden discs. *Steer horns* are also a favorite—saw off, fit wooden discs in the ends and tack with round-headed brass tacks.

Rawhide rattles are more difficult to make. Soak the hide, cut as shown and sew up. Fill with sand, place in the sun to dry, then shake out the sand and put in pebbles; insert the handle and bind with a wet rawhide thong.

RAWHIDE
-PLAINS-

TIN-CONE
-PLAINS-

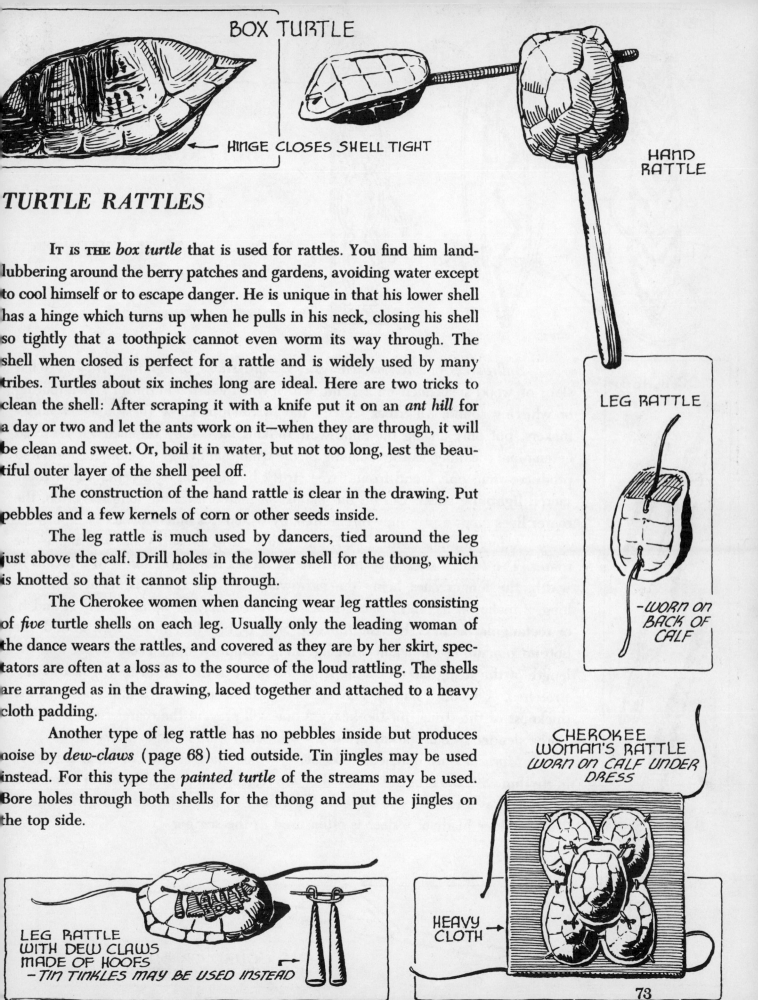

BOX TURTLE

← HINGE CLOSES SHELL TIGHT

HAND RATTLE

LEG RATTLE

—WORN ON BACK OF CALF

TURTLE RATTLES

IT IS THE *box turtle* that is used for rattles. You find him land-lubbering around the berry patches and gardens, avoiding water except to cool himself or to escape danger. He is unique in that his lower shell has a hinge which turns up when he pulls in his neck, closing his shell so tightly that a toothpick cannot even worm its way through. The shell when closed is perfect for a rattle and is widely used by many tribes. Turtles about six inches long are ideal. Here are two tricks to clean the shell: After scraping it with a knife put it on an *ant hill* for a day or two and let the ants work on it—when they are through, it will be clean and sweet. Or, boil it in water, but not too long, lest the beautiful outer layer of the shell peel off.

The construction of the hand rattle is clear in the drawing. Put pebbles and a few kernels of corn or other seeds inside.

The leg rattle is much used by dancers, tied around the leg just above the calf. Drill holes in the lower shell for the thong, which is knotted so that it cannot slip through.

The Cherokee women when dancing wear leg rattles consisting of *five* turtle shells on each leg. Usually only the leading woman of the dance wears the rattles, and covered as they are by her skirt, spectators are often at a loss as to the source of the loud rattling. The shells are arranged as in the drawing, laced together and attached to a heavy cloth padding.

Another type of leg rattle has no pebbles inside but produces noise by *dew-claws* (page 68) tied outside. Tin jingles may be used instead. For this type the *painted turtle* of the streams may be used. Bore holes through both shells for the thong and put the jingles on the top side.

CHEROKEE WOMAN'S RATTLE *WORN ON CALF UNDER DRESS*

HEAVY CLOTH →

LEG RATTLE WITH DEW CLAWS MADE OF HOOFS —*TIN TINKLES MAY BE USED INSTEAD*

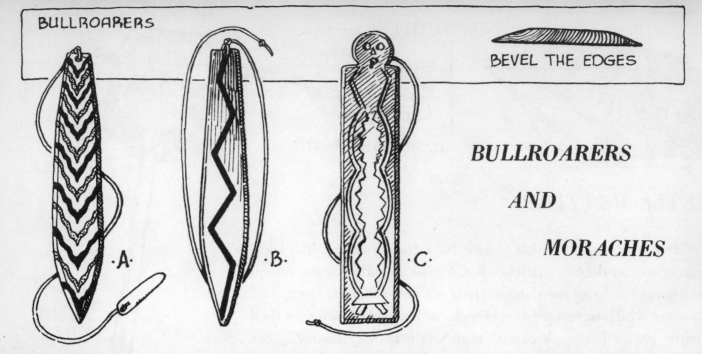

BEVEL THE EDGES

BULLROARERS
AND
MORACHES

Bullroarers, or *whizzers*, *whiz-sticks*, *whirr-sticks*, or *lightning-sticks*, are flat slabs of wood suspended on a string which when whirled in the air give a roaring or whirring sound. All tribes west of the Mississippi knew these ancient noise-makers, but only among the Southwest Indians have they retained their sacred ceremonial meaning, as the moaning of the wind that brings the thunderstorm and produces rain; only wood from a tree struck by lightning is acceptable for these sacred lightning sticks. But on the Plains, all sacred meaning long forgotten, the roarer lives on as a plaything of children, by whom it is much-loved.

A few minutes with a jackknife and a strip of softwood will make the roarer. The Indian sizes vary from 6 to 24 inches in length, and ½ to 2 inches in width, the longer ones being the narrower. The typical size is about 12 inches long, 2 inches wide, and ¼ inch thick. The roarer may be pointed as in A and B, or rectangular as in C, but the top side must be bevelled all the way around, the bottom remaining flat. Paint with lightning designs. Hopi custom has it that the length of the string should extend from the heart to the end of the right arm out-stretched. A wooden handle may be tied to the end. There is importance in the thickness of the string, for too heavy a one will prevent the roarer from whirring. Three slender strands loosely braided work better than a single heavy one.

Moraches are notched sticks along which another stick or bone is rubbed in rhythm with the drums. Usually they are rested on a gourd, basket or other hollow object as a resonator to increase the volume. Fifteen inches is a good length. The shoulder blade of a deer is often used as the scraper.

HALF GOURD OR BASKET
USED AS A RESONATOR

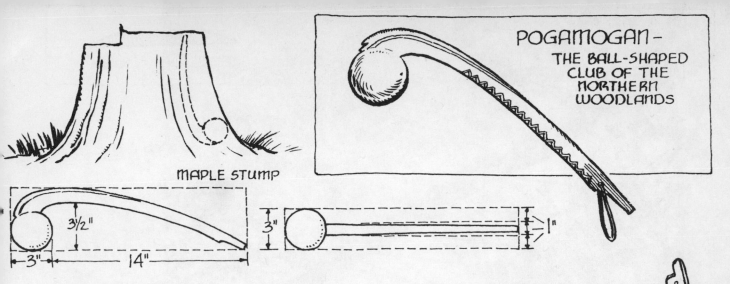

MAPLE STUMP

POGAMOGAN—
THE BALL-SHAPED CLUB OF THE NORTHERN WOODLANDS

3½"
3"
3"
14"
1"

WAR CLUBS

BEST-KNOWN IS THE *pogamogan* or ball-shaped club of the Woodlands. If for use only in dances it can be made of cedar or other softwood easy to work, but when made for business, hardwood was invariably sought. Find a big stump with out-curving roots and cut out a section as in the sketch. The wood is tough here, not apt to split, and the curve of the grain is right. When the club is shaped as in the drawings, round off and smooth the ball, scrape, sand, and polish with linseed oil. Decorate the handle with burnt etching (page 99).

The gun-shaped clubs show the white man's influence. Make it from a board and decorate with round-headed tacks. The iron spear-head may be imitated with wood, made separately and inserted.

Popular on the Plains is the stone club with rawhide covering. Cover both stone and wooden handle with wet rawhide which will shrink and hold solidly. The favorite rawhide is a bull's tail with the hair left on. The *slung-shot* club differs only in that the wooden handle is separated from the stone by two or three inches, thus leaving a flexible section of rawhide.

Stone clubs of hatchet shape are attached with rawhide as shown. Red pipestone is much used because it can be so easily worked.

GUN-SHAPED CLUB

¾" 3¼"
4½"
11"
2¼"
15"

PLAINS & WOODLANDS

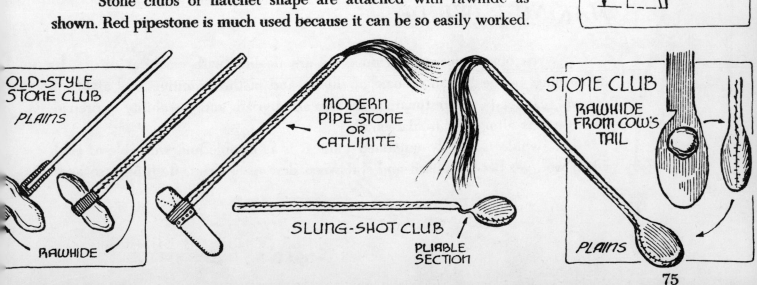

OLD-STYLE STONE CLUB

PLAINS

RAWHIDE

MODERN PIPE STONE OR CATLINITE

SLUNG-SHOT CLUB

PLIABLE SECTION

STONE CLUB

RAWHIDE FROM COW'S TAIL

PLAINS

MAKING RAWHIDE

WITH OUR HANDS ON RAWHIDE, we are dealing with essential things. Its importance in the Indian scheme of things, and in the primitive way of life in general, cannot be overestimated. Its uses are myriad, and the ability to prepare and use it is altogether fundamental.

Rawhide is merely untanned hide. It is as flexible and workable as cloth when wet, yet becomes hard and stiff when dry. As it dries, it shrinks, so as to

ROUND OFF EDGES

GRAINING POLE

BLOCK OF WOOD

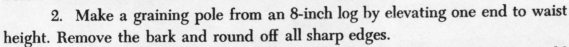

SCRAPER OR
GRAINING TOOL

2"

8"
20"

SECTION OF FILE
OR HACK BLADE

BUTCHER
KNIFE AS
SCRAPER

bind with great strength and tightness. Thongs of it are the Redman's wire, but is more versatile than wire in its flexibility and its shrinking and binding power.

1. Place the hide, whether green or dry, in a tub of lake or rain water for three or four days. If a green domestic hide is to be used, secure the hide (calf, sheep, or goat) the day the animal was killed if possible, and before it has been salted or treated with chemicals.

2. Make a graining pole from an 8-inch log by elevating one end to waist height. Remove the bark and round off all sharp edges.

3. Make a scraping tool as in the sketch, by inserting a piece of an old file in a slot cut in the stick, so that the edge projects ¼ inch. Round off the sharp corners at the ends. The back of a butcher knife will do in a pinch.

4. Place the hide, hair side up, on the graining pole and scrape off the hair and scarf skin by pushing away from you with scraper. Be careful not to rip or cut. A block of wood between the body and the hide protects the clothing.

5. If the hair does not slip readily, do not continue—sprinkle the hair side with wood ashes, then sprinkle well with water, roll up, wrap in wet burlap and let rest for three days longer. This is seldom necessary, however.

6. Turn the hide over and flesh it carefully with the scraper and a knife.

7. Wash thoroughly in soft water.

8. Place in a drying frame in a shady place and dry slowly. Make a vertical frame as in the sketch, or a horizontal one as in the photograph. In summer keep out of direct sun.

We now have rawhide. To turn it into buckskin, see the next chapter.

DRYING FRAME
- SET IN SHADY SPOT

MAKING BUCKSKIN

BUCKSKIN IS SOFTENED or Indian-tanned *deerskin,* although nowadays any kind of hide so prepared is often spoken of by that name. Buckskin is really not tanned at all, in that it is not treated chemically but is made pliable merely by rubbing it to break the fibers. Buckskin is as soft as any velvet, can be sewed like cloth, is exceedingly tough and strong for moccasins, windproof and warm for clothing.

No special talent is required to make good buckskin. The one indispensable ingredient is a willingness to labor long and unstintingly. If the following instructions are carefully followed, anyone can succeed who is of a mind to use the necessary muscle.

After the hide has been cleaned as for rawhide proceed as follows:

1. Soak the hide in soft water and stretch it very tightly in the frame.

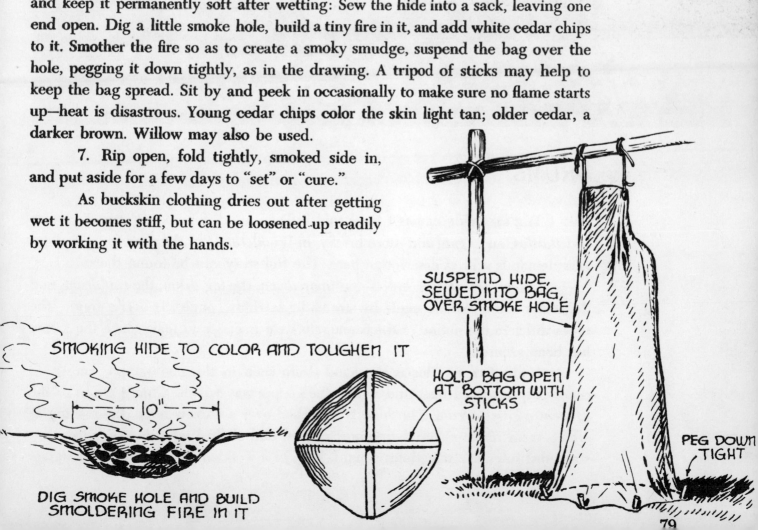

EDGE THIN AND SHARP 3" 24"

GRAINING or RUBBING STICK

2. Place the brains of the deer (or a calf's brains) in a little water and simmer a few minutes, then mash with the fingers to make a paste.

3. Rub the paste all over the hide on the hair side, rubbing it in with the palm of the hand, continuing rubbing until the hide is partly dry.

4. Put the hide in a pan with enough warm water to cover, rinse and churn it about with the hands. The water will become foamy and sudsy as if from soap. Catch a pocket of the water in the hide and squeeze it through; continue until it oozes through quickly and easily. Do this to all parts of the hide.

5. Wring the hide and stretch very tight in the frame. With a rubbing stick of hardwood (see sketch), the edge of which is thin and sharp, rub the hide with all possible muscle, covering every minute part of it on both sides, but concentrating on the hair side. You must work fast and hard, rubbing and rubbing until the skin is completely dry. Your hope of soft, velvety buckskin rests right here in this rubbing. If not soft enough, wet and repeat, or wrap the wet hide around a smooth post and pull back and forth with all your strength until dry.

6. Smoke the hide as follows, this to color it, close the pores, toughen it, and keep it permanently soft after wetting: Sew the hide into a sack, leaving one end open. Dig a little smoke hole, build a tiny fire in it, and add white cedar chips to it. Smother the fire so as to create a smoky smudge, suspend the bag over the hole, pegging it down tightly, as in the drawing. A tripod of sticks may help to keep the bag spread. Sit by and peek in occasionally to make sure no flame starts up—heat is disastrous. Young cedar chips color the skin light tan; older cedar, a darker brown. Willow may also be used.

7. Rip open, fold tightly, smoked side in, and put aside for a few days to "set" or "cure."

As buckskin clothing dries out after getting wet it becomes stiff, but can be loosened up readily by working it with the hands.

SMOKING HIDE TO COLOR AND TOUGHEN IT

10"

DIG SMOKE HOLE AND BUILD
SMOLDERING FIRE IN IT

SUSPEND HIDE,
SEWED INTO BAG,
OVER SMOKE HOLE

HOLD BAG OPEN
AT BOTTOM WITH
STICKS

PEG DOWN
TIGHT

DRUMS

THE STORY OF DRUMS I have told fully in another book, *Drums, Tomtoms and Rattles,* and again and more briefly, in *Woodcraft.* But the need for completeness demands a brief description here. The full story can be found there.

Drums are of four types—the *hoop drum,* the *log drum,* the *tub drum,* and the *water drum.* All are made by stretching rawhide (page 76) over a frame—the types differ in the nature of the frame. No item is easier to make once the frame has been secured.

Hoop Drum.—This is the hand drum seen in the photograph, known to practically all the tribes, and which the Chippewas call the *Chief's Drum* or the *Moccasin-game Drum.* The hide is stretched over a narrow hoop, the making of which from rustic materials requires careful and skillful whittling. For this reason substitutes are sometimes sought, such as a wooden mixing bowl, or a square

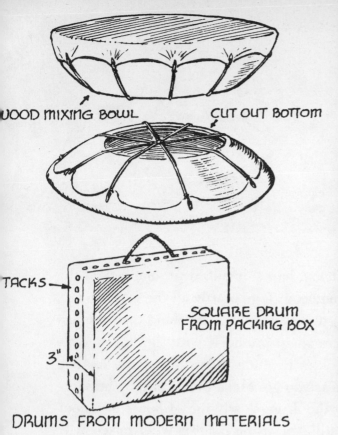

WOOD MIXING BOWL   CUT OUT BOTTOM

TACKS

3"

SQUARE DRUM
FROM PACKING BOX

DRUMS FROM MODERN MATERIALS

frame from a packing box, the latter being a modern version of the ancient square drum of the Plains. Make the hoop authentically if possible and produce a genuine drum.

Split the board from a straight-grained log of *white cedar* as shown. Shave down to ⅜ inch, soak for a day in water, and carefully bend into a hoop. Fasten the ends together with rawhide or wire. Stretch cords tightly crosswise of the hoop (see photograph) to hold in shape until it is dry and set. If necessary a hoop may be made from a round cheese box instead. These drums vary from 12 to 24 inches in diameter. The best ones are thin, never over three inches.

Soak the hide (deer, goat, or calf) for a

SPLIT OFF-
SHAVE TO ¼"
THICK

XX

2½"

18"

HOOP OF WHITE CEDAR

RAWHIDE LACING

XX

2½"

XX

XX

HOOP FROM CHEESE BOX - 2 LAYERS

TACK
HERE

HOOP DRUM

SINGLE HEAD

DOUBLE HEAD

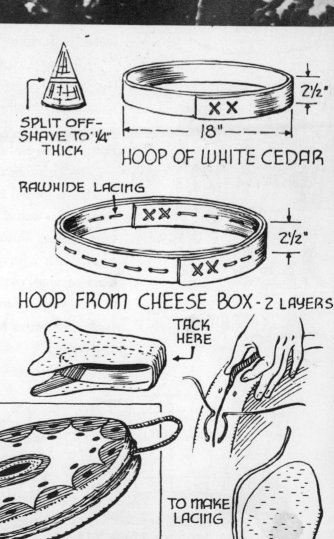

TO MAKE
LACING

81

COTTONWOOD
OR WHITE CEDAR
LOG

HOLLOW OUT WITH
CHISEL AND
MALLET

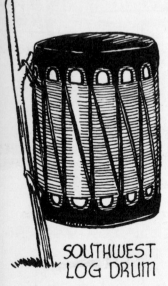

SOUTHWEST
LOG DRUM

full 24 hours. Lay it over the hoop, hair side out, drive one tack at the point shown, then tack the drumheads temporarily all the way around, each head as close to its own edge as possible, stretching the hide just tight enough so that it vibrates when thumped with the finger. Now lace the two together with a wet rawhide thong, using the method shown, withdrawing the tacks as you go. Make the handle by braiding three thongs, and tie on. Dry the drum slowly for 24 hours in a cool, shady place. Decorate while still wet, using paint powder mixed with water to form a paste.

Log Drums.—The Southwest Indians use cottonwood logs, but the white cedar of the Northwoods is better, having no equal for resonance. Hollow out carefully to make as thin a shell as possible. The hide is laced as shown, the edges scalloped out between the thongs. Paint the drumheads black and the log in colors.

Tub Drum.—The big dance drums of the Plains and Woodlands, thumped by a dozen drummers at once, are made over a *cedar wash tub—avoid those of other woods.* Use heavy hide, deer or calf, and lace as shown. In Chippewa style, paint one side red, the other blue, with a stripe across the middle in yellow edged with green. A skirt of wool cloth may cover the sides with red and blue to match.

Water Drum.—These are keg-shaped and contain three or four inches of water in the bottom, which gives the drum voice great carrying power.

SAW OUT BOTTOM 2" FROM EDGE
|← 24" →|

LARGE DANCE DRUM

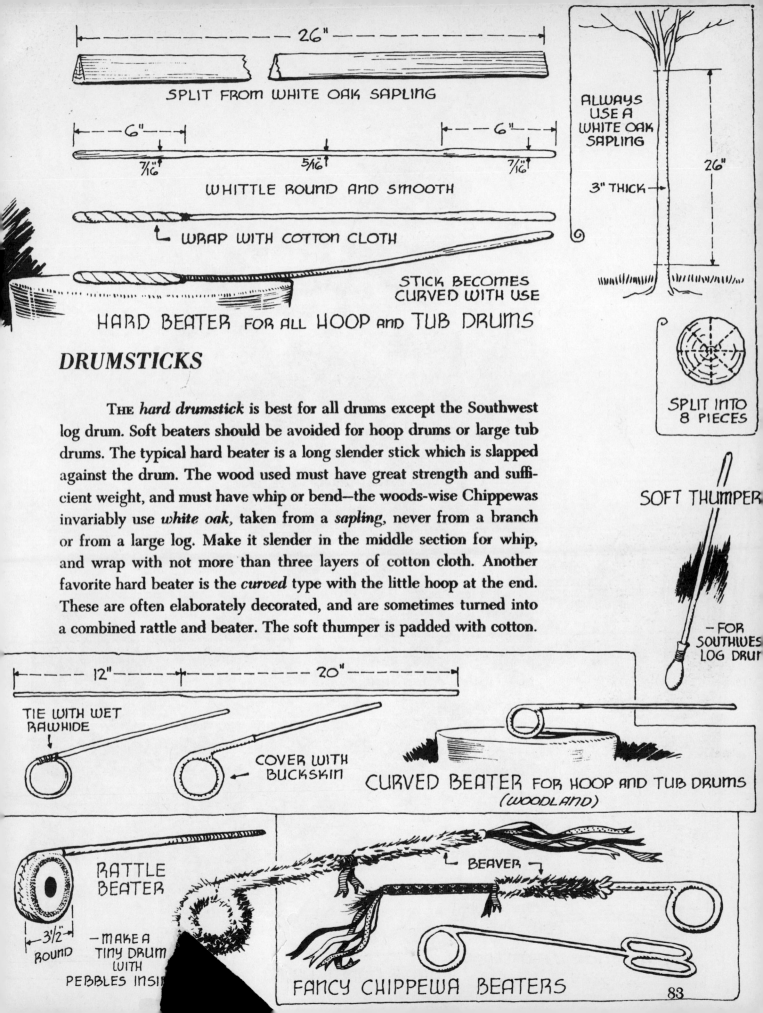

26"

SPLIT FROM WHITE OAK SAPLING

ALWAYS USE A WHITE OAK SAPLING

26"

3" THICK

6"   6"

7/16"   5/16"   7/16"

WHITTLE ROUND AND SMOOTH

WRAP WITH COTTON CLOTH

STICK BECOMES CURVED WITH USE

HARD BEATER FOR ALL HOOP AND TUB DRUMS

SPLIT INTO 8 PIECES

DRUMSTICKS

THE *hard drumstick* is best for all drums except the Southwest log drum. Soft beaters should be avoided for hoop drums or large tub drums. The typical hard beater is a long slender stick which is slapped against the drum. The wood used must have great strength and sufficient weight, and must have whip or bend—the woods-wise Chippewas invariably use *white oak,* taken from a *sapling*, never from a branch or from a large log. Make it slender in the middle section for whip, and wrap with not more than three layers of cotton cloth. Another favorite hard beater is the *curved* type with the little hoop at the end. These are often elaborately decorated, and are sometimes turned into a combined rattle and beater. The soft thumper is padded with cotton.

SOFT THUMPER

— FOR SOUTHWEST LOG DRUM

12"   20"

TIE WITH WET RAWHIDE

COVER WITH BUCKSKIN

CURVED BEATER FOR HOOP AND TUB DRUMS
(WOODLAND)

RATTLE BEATER

3½" ROUND

—MAKE A TINY DRUM WITH PEBBLES INSIDE

BEAVER

FANCY CHIPPEWA BEATERS

83

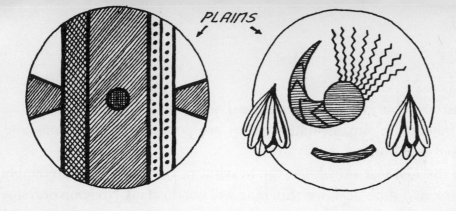

PLAINS

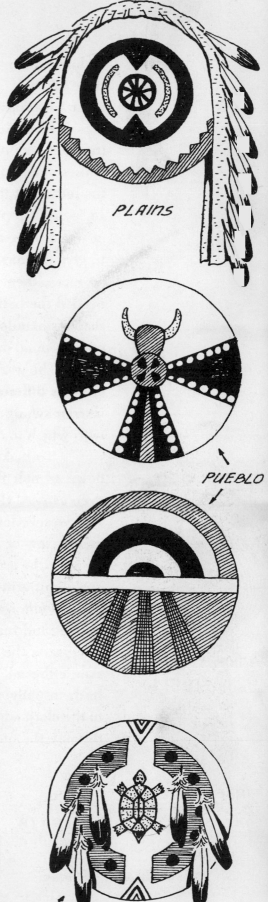

BUCKSKIN OR RED CLOTH

PLAINS

PUEBLO

SHIELDS

THUS IT WAS ON THE Plains: One's shield was the most valuable possession—his protection in battle, the conveyor of his medicine or spirit power. Made of the heaviest rawhide from the buffalo's shoulder, and shrunk to great thickness, it would ward off any spear or arrow, and ricochet any musket bullet. But more important were the medicine symbols adorning it, for verily they gave its owner uncommon fighting power, and certain guarantee of victory.

The shields carried by the horsemen of the Plains measured not more than 18 inches as a rule, for larger ones would encumber a rider. But among the foot-traveling Southwest warriors, 24 inches was the average size. In the Woodlands, shields were not used at all, because with the protection of trees and brush they were not needed, and more often than not would be a hindrance.

War shields were used only in fighting, and at other times reposed over the owner's bed or on a tripod in front of his tepee. For ceremonial use, as in dances, special shields were fashioned, resembling the real thing but made

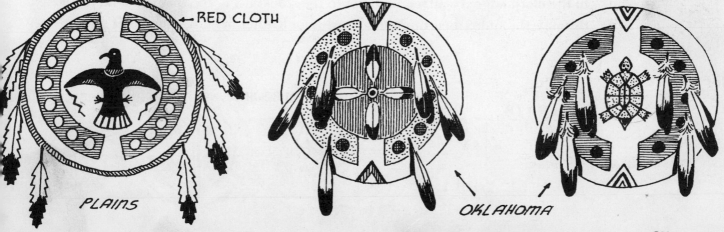

← RED CLOTH

PLAINS

OKLAHOMA

of buckskin light and thin. It is this ceremonial shield that has survived today, since its only function is ornamentation. They are popular as decorations and make unsurpassed wallhangings.

To make the real *war shield*, get the heaviest rawhide possible, preferably from a steer's neck and shoulders, for thin hide will not do at all. No hoop or frame is used, the shield relying for its strength solely on the stiffness and thickness of the hide. Cut it to twice the size of the shield desired, and soak it well. Dig a hole 18 inches deep and stake the hide over it. Roll hot stones into the hole and pour in water to create hot steam, thus shrinking and thickening the hide. It is possible to give it almost twice its original thickness in this way. Continue until it shrinks no more, then proceed at once, while it is still damp, to give it the convex shape needed the better to ward off missiles. Make a little mound of earth of the desired shape, stake down the hide over it, and leave in the sun until dry. Then trim the edges, pound out all wrinkles and rough spots, and decorate.

The war shield of the Plains was covered with thin buckskin decorated with symbols different from those on the shield proper, which was removed just as the warrior swung into battle, to reveal the real medicine symbols on the shield itself, with which to confound the enemy.

To make a *dance shield*, use a barrel hoop as a frame, the wood whittled down to half its usual width. Cover it with thin rawhide, buckskin, chamois, or even canvas. If rawhide, wet the hide and lace across the backside as in the drawing, loosely lest the hide warp the hoop when it dries. If buckskin or canvas, merely sew or lace the folds along the edge around the backside as in the sketch. Arrange the arm straps as illustrated so that, when the shield is slipped on the left arm, both arm and hand are free for action.

Paint the design with water-color poster paint and cover with white shellac to fix it and tone down the brightness. Always use flat colors. Follow the types of designs on the preceding page. Shields are often edged with red flannel or buckskin, either all the way around or with the ends left hanging. Feathers of fighting birds, usually short eagle quills, are often attached, either to the shield proper or to the cloth edge. In attaching them to the shield itself, the thong should be passed through the hide, then through a washer of leather behind, to prevent pulling out.

ARM STRAPS
WAR SHIELD
– OF HEAVY
RAWHIDE

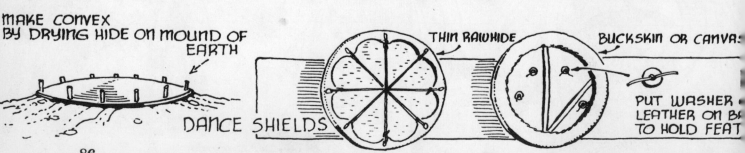

MAKE CONVEX
BY DRYING HIDE ON MOUND OF
EARTH

THIN RAWHIDE

BUCKSKIN OR CANVAS

DANCE SHIELDS

PUT WASHER
LEATHER ON B
TO HOLD FEAT

SPEAR

HORSEHAIR

BANNER OR INDIAN "FLAG"

COUP-STICKS AND SPEARS

A *coup-stick* is a long slender staff resembling a spear but lacking the business end of the spear. It is an *honor stick*, used for "counting coup" in battle, that is, for striking an enemy, and as such was harmless, for the highest honor went to him, not who killed, but who touched a living enemy with hand or harmless stick.

The spear with its flint point is seen at the top, six or more feet long. For ceremonial use, as in dances, the point is often of wood, and among the Chippewas is often barbed as in the upper corner.

Coup-sticks are of many types, but all are made of light, slender sticks about ¾ inch thick. The banner type, much loved as a battle flag, consists of eagle or other fighting-bird feathers, prepared as for a war-bonnet and laced to a strip of felt, which is folded over the stick as in the upper corner, or attached at the ends only as at the bottom. This arrangement is also often used on dance spears.

Most famous of coup-sticks is the *dog-soldier staff*, symbol of the highest of the high among fighting men, carried by the unconquerable dog-soldiers of the Plains. It has a crooked end and is covered with otter or other fur, cut in strips and wrapped on, bandage-fashion. Use black ash for the stick, soak it for a day, heat the end in a fire, and bend very cautiously.

COUP-STICKS

COUP-STICK
BANNER TYPE

DOG-SOLDIER STAFF →

WOLF TAIL

OTTER FUR

87

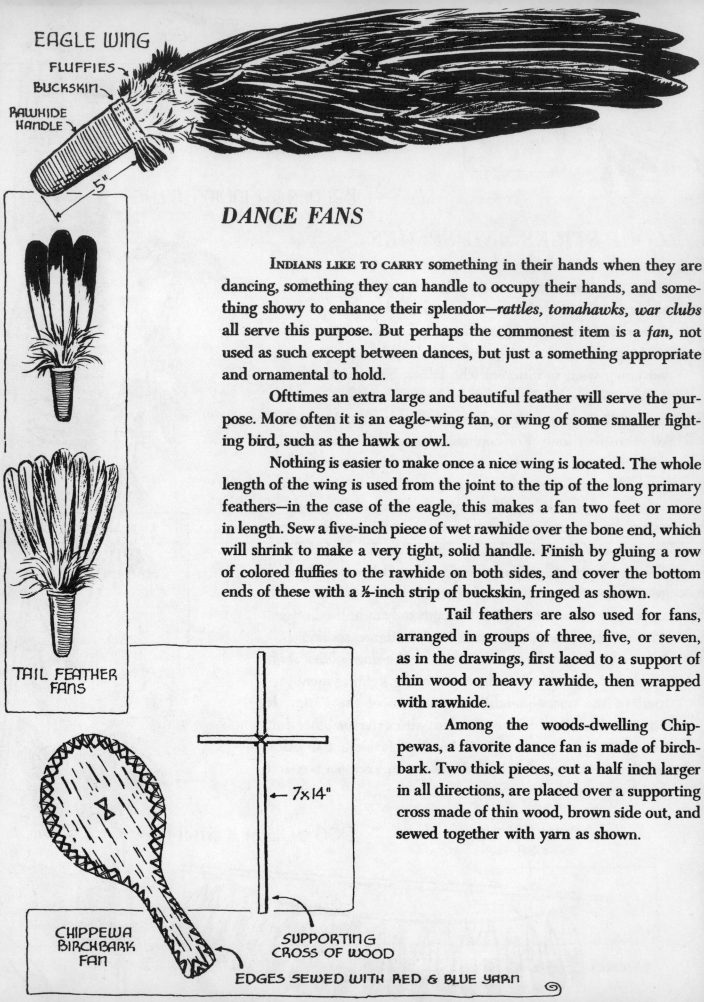

EAGLE WING

FLUFFIES

BUCKSKIN

RAWHIDE HANDLE

5"

DANCE FANS

INDIANS LIKE TO CARRY something in their hands when they are dancing, something they can handle to occupy their hands, and something showy to enhance their splendor—*rattles, tomahawks, war clubs* all serve this purpose. But perhaps the commonest item is a *fan*, not used as such except between dances, but just a something appropriate and ornamental to hold.

Ofttimes an extra large and beautiful feather will serve the purpose. More often it is an eagle-wing fan, or wing of some smaller fighting bird, such as the hawk or owl.

Nothing is easier to make once a nice wing is located. The whole length of the wing is used from the joint to the tip of the long primary feathers—in the case of the eagle, this makes a fan two feet or more in length. Sew a five-inch piece of wet rawhide over the bone end, which will shrink to make a very tight, solid handle. Finish by gluing a row of colored fluffies to the rawhide on both sides, and cover the bottom ends of these with a ½-inch strip of buckskin, fringed as shown.

Tail feathers are also used for fans, arranged in groups of three, five, or seven, as in the drawings, first laced to a support of thin wood or heavy rawhide, then wrapped with rawhide.

Among the woods-dwelling Chippewas, a favorite dance fan is made of birchbark. Two thick pieces, cut a half inch larger in all directions, are placed over a supporting cross made of thin wood, brown side out, and sewed together with yarn as shown.

TAIL FEATHER FANS

7x14"

CHIPPEWA BIRCHBARK FAN

SUPPORTING CROSS OF WOOD

EDGES SEWED WITH RED & BLUE YARN

ORNAMENTAL FEATHERS

THESE ARE MADE OF several feathers pieced together to make one mighty one, bigger than any feather of its type that ever grew. They are used primarily as hand ornaments serving the same purpose as fans, and as such they are effective indeed. They never fail to cause speculation as to their source.

Several feathers are needed of approximately the same size and shape, and of the same color and mottling. Dark eagle feathers are excellent, and all-white are also used. The larger the quills the sturdier the resulting feather will be.

Cut the shaft of one of the feathers at the middle with a safety-razor blade, being careful not to cut or mar the web. The top half of this is to be the tip of our overgrown feather, and the bottom half its butt. Now cut out the middle sections of three or four feathers with which to make the center of the long quill. These sections should measure three to four inches, for if longer the big quill may not have the proper curve. Lay the sections out in order, and then shorten and adjust them as need be to make a nice, natural-looking feather.

The sections are attached by forcing a short plug of wood into the adjoining ends of the shafts. Where the shafts are hollow, use a matchstick whittled down to fit and well covered with airplane glue; when solid, force a glued toothpick into them. When the web is fingered at the intersections it will attach itself so as to remove all evidence of being pieced together. The edges are then trimmed uniformly with scissors.

Insert a six-inch stick into the butt end for a handle and add tip and butt fluffies as shown. The feather is now attractive enough, but the Karaks would add a ⅜-inch beaded strip to the shaft as shown, sewing it with thread at intervals.

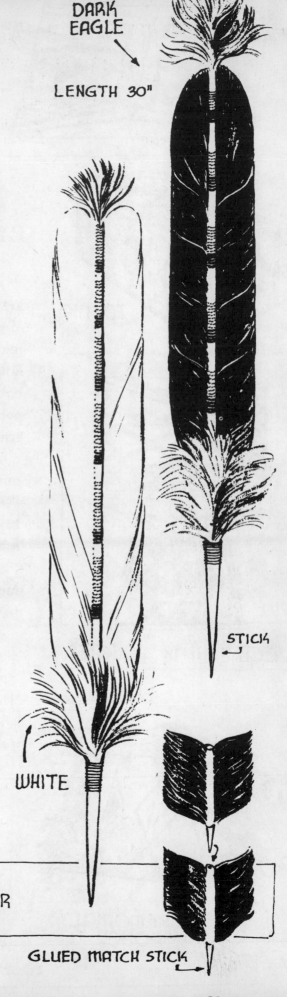

DARK EAGLE

LENGTH 30"

STICK

WHITE

GLUED MATCH STICK

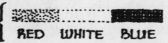

SEVERAL SECTIONS OF FEATHERS PIECED TOGETHER TO MAKE ONE LARGE ONE

BEADING COLORS { RED WHITE BLUE

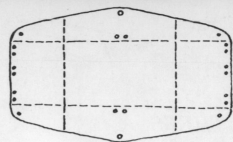
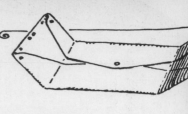

PARFLECHE

TRUNK

RECTANGULAR POUCHES

PARFLECHE OF THE PLAINS

THE NAME IS OF French origin and refers to the rawhide car
ing case shown at the top of the page. It is made of a rectangular pi
of rawhide, square at the ends but irregular at the sides. The sides
folded first, then the ends, to make a sort of huge envelope. There
holes through which the ends are tied together. The folds are round
not squarely bent, so as to permit expansion to fit the contents. '
pattern above is for an envelope of typical shape, its length ab
twice that of its width. With an average size of 1 by 2 feet, parflec
range from 1 to 3 feet long, and 6 to 18 inches wide. There are
miniature ones of pocket size.

The trunk is made of rawhide cut to the pattern, folded
laced or sewed with sinew. In size these correspond to parfleches, v
a height of one foot.

The pouches are seen in all shapes and sizes from six to eight
inches. The cylindrical case is for crushable articles, particul
feathers.

All of these articles are decorated in a characteristic type of
sign, often referred to as parfleche decoration. It is characterized
simple geometric patterns, large and bold and free from small de
The drawings indicate the type. Use water colors with a little
added as a fixative and apply flat, without shading. Colors are
yellow, blue, green, brown, and black.

CEREMONIAL
POUCH

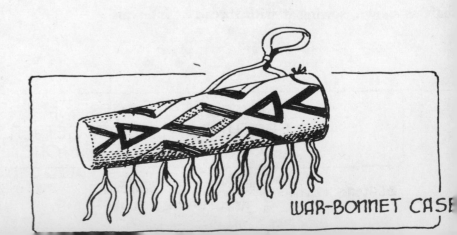

WAR-BONNET CASE

TRUNK

LACE ON LIDS

PACKING BASKETS

WOODEN HANDLE

MAKUKS

SHOULDER STRAP

BIRCHBARK OF THE WOODS

In the Northwoods, the parfleche of the Plains gives way to the matchless bark of the white birch. Strong, pliable, leathery, it fulfills all the functions of parfleche and in much the same way. Never strip the bark from a live birch tree unless far back in the uninhabited wilds—*use bark from a down tree*.

Birchbark is usually fashioned into *makuks* (baskets), but is sometimes folded into a temporary trunk as at the top. For pack-baskets a lid may be laced on, but usually the basket is left open.

A wooden hoop fashioned by whittling and bending a branch is laced to the top of the basket, on the outside, to give it rigidity. The bark is cut to a cardboard pattern, folded and laced as in the drawing. For lacing, the inner bark of basswood is used. Birchbark is always placed with the *inner* or *brown side* out.

Birchbark is decorated by etching it—draw the design with a pencil, then scrape off the thin layer of dark bark around the design so that the design stands out dark against a lighter background.

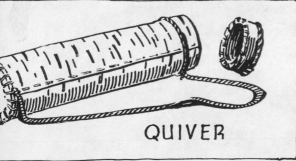

QUIVER

WOODEN TOP & BOTTOM

HOOP AROUND TOP

PATTERN OF CARDBOARD

ALL LACINGS ARE OF BASSWOOD BARK

ETCHED DESIGN BY SCRAPING OFF DARK OUTER LAYER

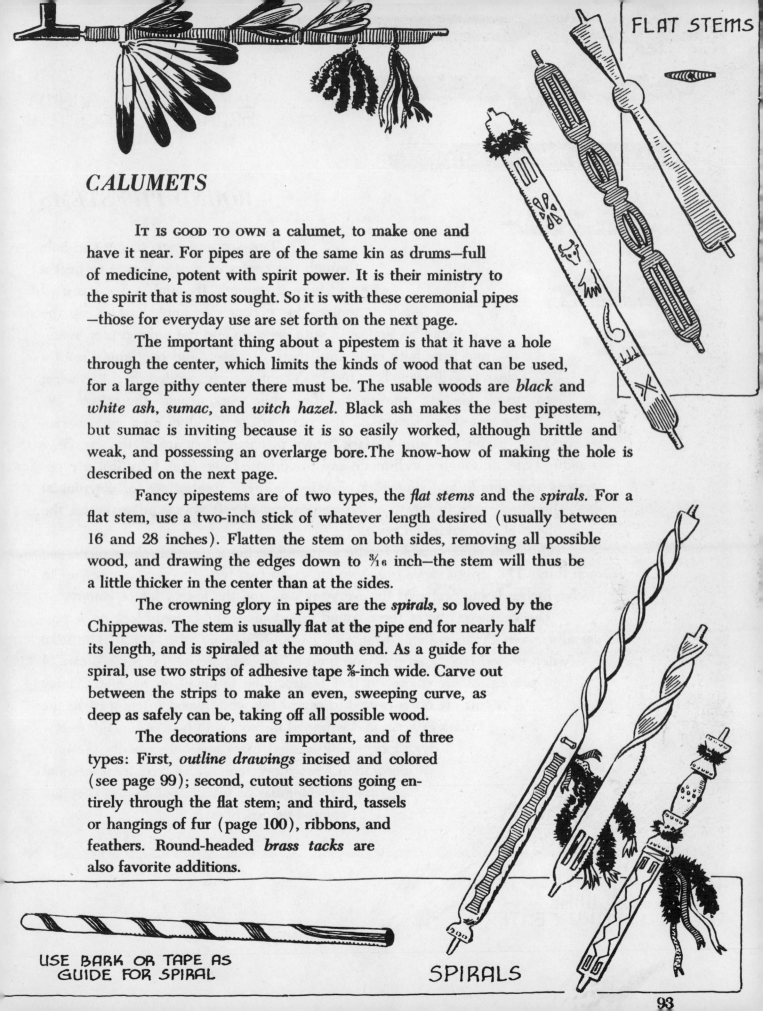

CALUMETS

IT IS GOOD TO OWN a calumet, to make one and
have it near. For pipes are of the same kin as drums—full
of medicine, potent with spirit power. It is their ministry to
the spirit that is most sought. So it is with these ceremonial pipes
—those for everyday use are set forth on the next page.

The important thing about a pipestem is that it have a hole
through the center, which limits the kinds of wood that can be used,
for a large pithy center there must be. The usable woods are *black* and
white ash, *sumac*, and *witch hazel*. Black ash makes the best pipestem,
but sumac is inviting because it is so easily worked, although brittle and
weak, and possessing an overlarge bore. The know-how of making the hole is
described on the next page.

Fancy pipestems are of two types, the *flat stems* and the *spirals*. For a
flat stem, use a two-inch stick of whatever length desired (usually between
16 and 28 inches). Flatten the stem on both sides, removing all possible
wood, and drawing the edges down to ³/₁₆ inch—the stem will thus be
a little thicker in the center than at the sides.

The crowning glory in pipes are the *spirals*, so loved by the
Chippewas. The stem is usually flat at the pipe end for nearly half
its length, and is spiraled at the mouth end. As a guide for the
spiral, use two strips of adhesive tape ⅜-inch wide. Carve out
between the strips to make an even, sweeping curve, as
deep as safely can be, taking off all possible wood.

The decorations are important, and of three
types: First, *outline drawings* incised and colored
(see page 99); second, cutout sections going entirely through the flat stem; and third, tassels
or hangings of fur (page 100), ribbons, and
feathers. Round-headed *brass tacks* are
also favorite additions.

USE BARK OR TAPE AS
GUIDE FOR SPIRAL

SPIRALS

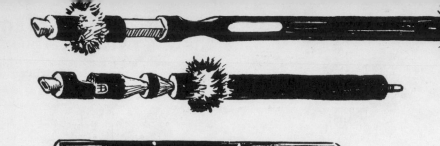

ROUND PIPESTEMS

THE METHOD USED to get the hole
through the center of a pipestem is to heat a
wire and burn it through. If suitable wood is used
—ash or sumac—this becomes a simple task. Keep the
wire hot and push with pressure into the pithy center, ream-
ing from both ends until the holes meet, and continuing until a
clean free-drawing bore results. The process is speeded up if two wires
are used, keeping one in the fire while working with the other.

The pipestems shown on the page are of a widely used and characteristic type, round and burned dark brown in color. They are of the everyday
smoking type, although a well-made and ornamented one is as beautiful a pipestem as any, simple and altogether effective, entirely appropriate for ceremonial
use. They are made in the true and ancient woodcraft way, and carry all the
atmosphere of the wildwood peoples.

Only ash is acceptable for these items. Secure a straight, clean piece one
inch thick. The length varies from two inches to two feet, the shorter ones up to
twelve inches being preferred for everyday use, and the longer for ceremony.

The characteristic of these round pipestems is the brown-black color universally given them, without which they would be in no wise typical. The stem
when peeled is greased well and held in the campfire until it turns brown, a
process of fire coloration that is described in detail on page 98. Fancy
stems are often carved to reveal the white wood in contrast to the
dark exterior, and wrapped in spots with beaver fur. For everyday pipes, round-headed brass tacks are usually the only
decoration. Very short stems of this type are sometimes
made rectangular or square, but always they are
colored as described.

TO PUT THE
HOLE THROUGH,
FORCE HOT WIRE
THROUGH PITHY CENTER

94

PIPE-TOMAHAWKS

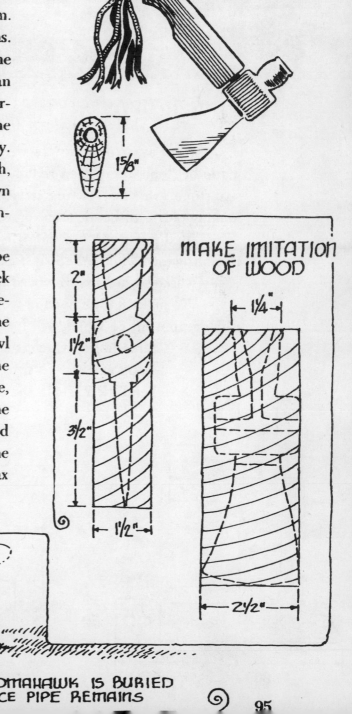

TOMAHAWK PIPE
ENGLISH TRADER
TYPE

METAL

1⅝"

THE PIPE OF PEACE—such is the pipe-tomahawk—the pipe from which the phrase "burying the tomahawk" arose. Combination of the symbol of war and the symbol of peace, it is at once a functioning tomahawk and a functioning pipe, the pipe bowl being in the pole of the ax, and the ax handle serving as the stem. The hatchet buried, only the symbol of peace remains.

The pipe-tomahawk was popularized by the early white traders, made especially for the Indian trade, the English, French, and Spaniards each featuring a style of their own. That in the drawing is the English type, still common in the Indian country today.

The handle, like all pipestems, is made of ash, in this case from a two-inch piece, shaped as shown in the cross-section, and decorated by the usual methods as described for other pipestems.

An imitation of the pipe-tomahawk can be made of wood by following the diagrams. Cut a block of clear softwood to the dimensions indicated, and before shaping it drill the holes as indicated by the dotted lines with a half-inch bit. Then enlarge the bowl with a knife to a ¾-inch diameter at the top. When the tomahawk is whittled to shape, fit the handle in place, insert a pencil in the bowl and mark the outline of the hole on the handle. Then withdraw the handle and cut the hole as marked on it, so as to connect with the bore. Make the handle secure with glue. Paint the ax head in imitation of brass or copper.

MAKE IMITATION
OF WOOD

2"

1½"

3½"

1½"

1¼"

2½"

WHEN THE TOMAHAWK IS BURIED
THE PEACE PIPE REMAINS

PIPE BOWLS

THE BEAUTIFUL BOWLS we think of in connection with Indian pipes are made of stone, the prized red ones of pipestone (*catlinite*) and the black ones of soapstone (*steatite*). While serviceable imitations can be fashioned of wood, the making of the authentic stone ones is easier than one might think.

Red pipestone (*catlinite*) is still obtained from the ancient Indian quarries in southwest Minnesota. Soapstone is common in many areas. Both are soft and easily worked when first removed but soon harden to make work more difficult.

To make a pipe bowl of wood, select the shape desired from those in the photograph, all of which are Indian-made stone bowls except the one with the three holes, which is a wooden imitation. Secure a block of clear soft-wood and cut to size (the one in the photograph was made from a hemlock 2 x 4). Draw the outline on it and before shaping it, drill

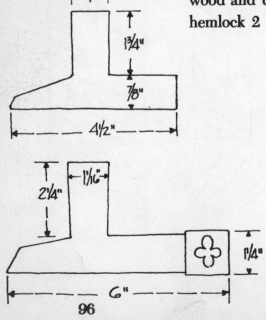

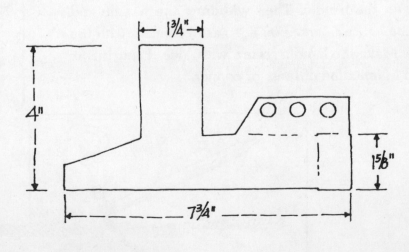

the holes with a ½-inch bit, enlarging the hole in the bowl cone-shaped with a jack-knife. Shape the bowl roughly with a saw and then proceed with knife and wood rasp. Sand carefully and rub with a coarse cloth until smooth and shiny. Paint red, using dry paint powder mixed with water to make a paste, into which a little liquid glue is poured. The glue not only fixes the paint but gives the needed slight gloss. Always avoid lacquer and oil paint.

Stone bowls are made in the same way, using hacksaws and metal drills for cutting, and files for smoothing. Polish with emery cloth and melted beeswax. The inlaid designs are of melted lead.

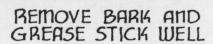

REMOVE BARK AND GREASE STICK WELL

HOLD OVER FIRE OF GREEN HARDWOOD

RUB WITH COARSE CLOTH WHILE STILL HOT

STICK IS NOW DARK BROWN OR BLACK

DECORATE BY CARVING TO SHOW WHITE WOOD

OR
↓

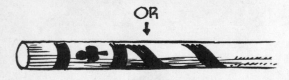

LEAVE BARK DESIGN, THEN

↓

AFTER HEATING, REMOVE BARK TO SHOW WHITE DESIGN

FIRE COLORATION

TRULY THE HAND of the primitive is on it, the spirit of the wildwood within it, when naught but the smoke of the burning campfire is used to color it. No paints, no dyes, no foreign coloring of any type—here is the most ancient and primal of all the means of adorning wood. Stems so treated have that unmistakably Indian atmosphere.

This is the method by which the round pipe-stems on page 94 are given their characteristic appearance. Dishes, too, and other wooden items of many types are so treated. It was from the Chippewas of the Northwoods that I first learned it, and since have seen evidences of it in many museums.

Let us suppose it is an ash pipestem: First remove the bark and grease it well and thoroughly with any kind of animal grease. Then hold it in a campfire of green hardwood, heating it evenly all over. When turned uniformly dark of the desired shade, withdraw and *before it cools* rub it briskly with a coarse cloth, producing a smooth shiny surface of brown ranging from medium to dark approaching black, depending on the length of time in the fire. The dark shades are preferred.

There are two ways to add highlights: The first is to carve the stick in spots, as seen on the pipestems on page 94. The white wood thus exposed stands out with such virgin purity against the dark that merely to handle it seems out of place. A touch of yellow water color here and there on the white is delightful, but other colors should be avoided.

The second method of adornment is to leave the bark attached in spots, trimmed carefully to the desired design, and removing all bark elsewhere. After heating, the remaining bark is removed to reveal the pure white design beneath. This can also be reversed, making dark designs on white.

BURNT ETCHING

THIS METHOD OF engraving by heat is again one of the most ancient of the Redman's arts, having been practiced for—we know not how many centuries. It is so simple any child can handle it, yet when properly done and with correct designs, it gives to any wood object that characteristic flavor that is known as Indian. It has long been a favorite method of adorning pipestems and similar small objects.

Simple *point engraving* was a widely used Indian means of decorating wood, which consists of merely scratching the design with a pointed tool so as to make indentations or depressed lines. *Burnt etching* is similar except that a heated metal point is used so as to burn the line, thus making it more distinct.

First draw the design with pencil, then, using a wire or a pointed tool such as an ice pick, heat the point and retrace the pencil lines. The result is a burnt outline, both indented in the wood and black or brown in color. Often it is left as is, but if color is desired, the lines are scraped with a cold point to remove the black, and the indentations then filled with water color.

In this way the flat pipestems on page 93 were decorated, which should be studied for appropriate designs. Note that color is used sparingly, in the outlines only, seldom solidly over the whole design. Avoid all civilized symbols, and adhere strictly to Indian motifs. Effort to "improve" on Indian designs are seldom if ever rewarding. It is better to copy and be authentic than to improvise and lose the Indian effect.

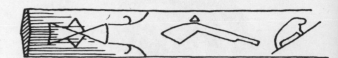

DRAW DESIGN WITH PENCIL

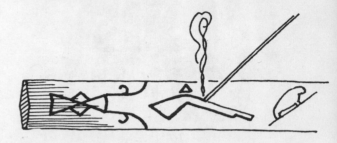

BURN LINES WITH HOT WIRE

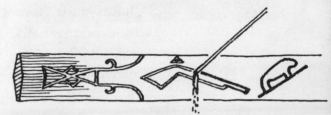

TO COLOR, SCRAPE OFF BLACK WITH COLD WIRE

THEN FILL INDENTATIONS WITH COLOR WITH SPLINTER OF WOOD

FUR TASSELS

WE SEE THEM ON pipestems, on the sides of drums, on drumsticks, on tomahawks, on war-bonnets and turbans—and always they are among the most loved of adornments, particularly in the northern Woodlands where fur is plentiful.

To those unfamiliar with Indian ways, the how of making these fur tassels is often puzzling, since close examination reveals that no thread holds them together. The trick is this: They are made of *raw* hide, merely cleaned and dried with the fur on, not tanned or treated in any way. The hide is then cut into strips ¾-inch wide and soaked in water. A string is tied to each end of the strip, and the hide then twisted into the form of a tassel. The strings are then tied between two upright supports so as to stretch the fur tightly, where is remains for 24 hours until thoroughly dry. When the strings are removed the tassel remains twisted permanently. By rubbing with the hands, the fur is brought back to its original fluffiness.

Ten inches is the usual length, and four to six tassels are needed to make a cluster. At the bottom end of each tassel, two short colored ribbons should be sewed as shown.

Among the Chippewas who make greatest use of these tassels, *beaver* is the fur invariably used, while *otter* is preferred on the Plains, Any untanned fur will do. *Weasel* can be prepared in this way for the white tassels so loved by the Blackfeet for side hangings on their war-bonnets.

A cluster of these tassels is often attached to the middle of a pipestem as shown above, or to each side of a hoop drum that is edged with fur, such as that seen on page 80. They are appropriate whenever hangings are appropriate.

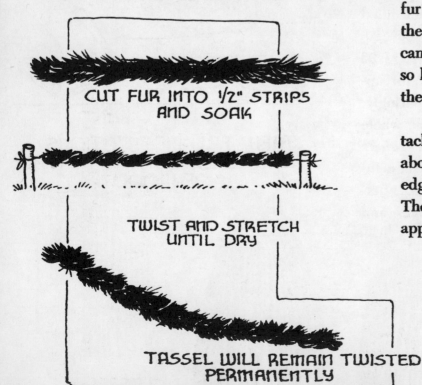

CUT FUR INTO ½" STRIPS AND SOAK

TWIST AND STRETCH UNTIL DRY

TASSEL WILL REMAIN TWISTED PERMANENTLY

YARN
POMPONS
AND
TASSELS

INDIANS LOVE YARN and use it in many interesting and unusual ways. Although a modern material, it nevertheless seems to add a primitive touch and an undeniable Indian flavor. Its use is always appropriate.

Pompons, the little round balls of yarn, are popular at the ends of rows of wooden beads, often set in a thimble or a tin cone—such strings of beads are much used on the skirts of large dance drums. Pompons are also used at the ends of beaded arm-bands, leg-bands and belts, at the rear end of roaches, and indeed wherever hangings are appropriate. Tassels are employed where longer hangings are needed.

Pompons and tassels as made in the Indian country are in nowise different from those made elsewhere. The pompons are about an inch in diameter and are usually made of two colors of yarn mixed, such as red and blue, or red and yellow. Lay a number of short strands on top each other, the two colors mixed, then pull together tightly at the middle with stout thread and tie. Trim the ends of the yarn until a perfectly round ball results. Tassels are tied in the same way, the strands being longer, and an added tie made near the top.

POMPON

THREAD

YARN

TIE TIGHTLY AND TRIM YARN TO MAKE ROUND BALL

YARN →

THREAD TIED TIGHTLY

TIE WITH YARN HERE →

·C·

·B·

·A·

TASSEL

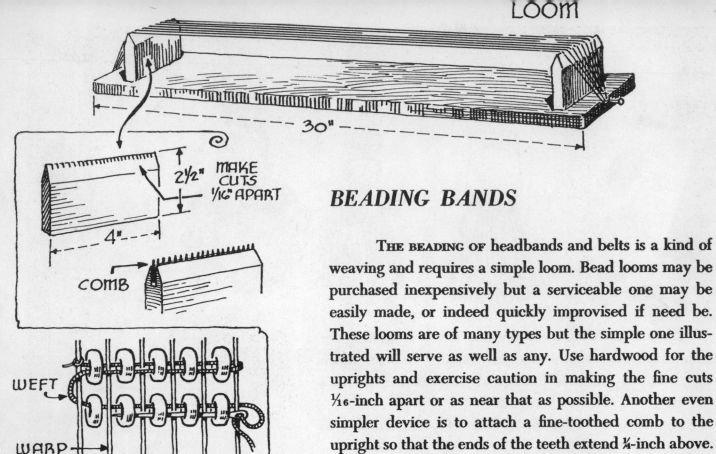

BEADING BANDS

THE BEADING OF headbands and belts is a kind of weaving and requires a simple loom. Bead looms may be purchased inexpensively but a serviceable one may be easily made, or indeed quickly improvised if need be. These looms are of many types but the simple one illustrated will serve as well as any. Use hardwood for the uprights and exercise caution in making the fine cuts ⅟₁₆-inch apart or as near that as possible. Another even simpler device is to attach a fine-toothed comb to the upright so that the ends of the teeth extend ¼-inch above.

Linen thread well-waxed should be used in preference to cotton when possible. Stretch the warp thread tightly in the frame as shown. There should be one more thread than the number of beads required. *Always use an odd number of beads,* such as 11, 17, and 25, in order that there be a middle row with an equal number of beads on each side of it, this to make the geometric designs come out right.

Set the loom so that it extends away from you, start at the far end, and work toward you. Thread the bead needle, tie the end of the thread to the warp thread on the left side, and bring the thread out to the right under the warp. Run the needle through the required numberof beads and space them under the warp, setting the beads so that one appears between each two threads. Place the left forefinger under the beads to hold them and then run the needle back through the beads, this time on top of the warp. Now go underneath for the next row. Opaque glass beads are the best, although transparent ones are sometimes used. Browbands are about 1¼ inches wide and require about 21 beads per row. See page 13 for typical designs. The easiest way to lay out the design is on a sheet of squared paper, allowing one square per bead. The resulting design will not be accurate since the beads are wider than they are thick but it will provide a working diagram.

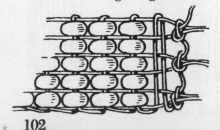

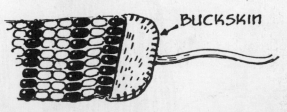

WOODLAND BEADING

FOR APPLYING BEADS directly to buckskin or cloth, the *overlaid stitch* was known and used by Indians in all parts of the country, although the Plains tribes developed and made greater use of another and easier method called the *lazy stitch* which was better suited to their geometric patterns. The overlaid stitch is particularly well adapted for curves, and therefore is ideal for flower patterns; it was used exclusively by the Woodland tribes for the floral designs for which they are justly famous.

In the overlaid stitch, two threads are used, the bead thread on which the beads are strung, and the sewing thread with which the bead thread is stitched to the buckskin or cloth. The end of the bead thread is attached to the buckskin and then a few beads are strung on it and laid on the buckskin. Then the sewing thread is stitched over the bead thread at right angles to it, as shown in the drawing. More beads are then strung on the thread and put in place, and the sewing thread run along through the buckskin under them, when it emerges to make another stitch. In sewing on the buckskin, the sewing thread never goes entirely through but is run along just below the surface, as indicated by the dotted line, so that no stitches show on the wrong side. In the case of cloth, however, which is less firm, the stitch goes entirely through.

The number of beads used between the stitches depends upon the pattern or design. In straight rows of the same color, there may be as many as six or eight. Whenever the color changes there should be a stitch. On curves, no more than two or three are used. On moccasins where the beading receives rough usage, there should be a stitch for each one or two beads.

In over-all beading, as on the beautiful Chippewa medicine bag in the photograph, the floral designs are applied first, then the white background is added with the beads in straight rows.

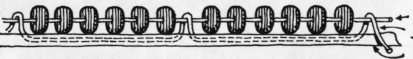

← BEAD THREAD
SEWING THREAD
BUCKSKIN

FOR STRAIGHT LINES — 6 TO 8 BEADS

FOR CURVES AND FINE WORK — 2 TO 3 BEADS

OVERLAID STITCH

FOR MOCCASINS — 1 BEAD

PLAINS BEADING

IN THE SIOUX COUNTRY of the northern Plains where geometric patterns were the vogue, the *lazy stitch* was developed to simplify and reduce the labor of beading, and yet to produce a most pleasing effect. The absence of curves in these designs made possible the change from the tedious overlaid stitch. One glance at a piece of lazy work will label it as from the prairie country.

First, fasten one end of the bead thread to the buckskin, then string a number of beads on the thread. Make a stitch at the end of the row of beads, attaching the thread to the skin. Now string the same number of beads on the thread and bring it back parallel to the first and make another stitch. The pattern is thus built up of rows of beads attached at the ends of the rows only. The number of beads may vary from 6 to 12, but seldom more than 8 are used.

A fine awl is needed to perforate the skin before the needle is passed through lest many needles be broken. The thread does not go all the way through the skin but runs beneath the surface so that no stitches can be seen. As a substitute for the sinew used as thread by the Indians, fine linen thread, well-waxed, is needed. The lazy stitch tends to pull out unless firmly stitched, and the thread tends to break if weak. For use on cloth, the Indians prefer to put the beads on buckskin and then sew it to the cloth. If applying directly to cloth, the cloth should be backed with other material to provide a firm base.

It will be noted that each row of beads tends to bulge or arch outward a little so that the beading appears in rows of ridges, as can be seen on the waist in the photograph. This gives a certain rhythm to the beading, and is a quickly spotted label that identifies Plains work. The difference can be seen by comparing the waist in this photograph with the flat beading of the medicine bag on the preceding page done with the overlaid stitch.

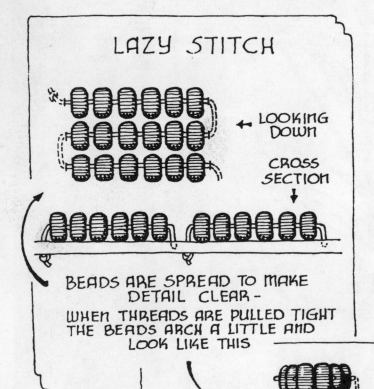

LAZY STITCH

← LOOKING DOWN

CROSS SECTION ↓

BEADS ARE SPREAD TO MAKE DETAIL CLEAR —
WHEN THREADS ARE PULLED TIGHT THE BEADS ARCH A LITTLE AND LOOK LIKE THIS

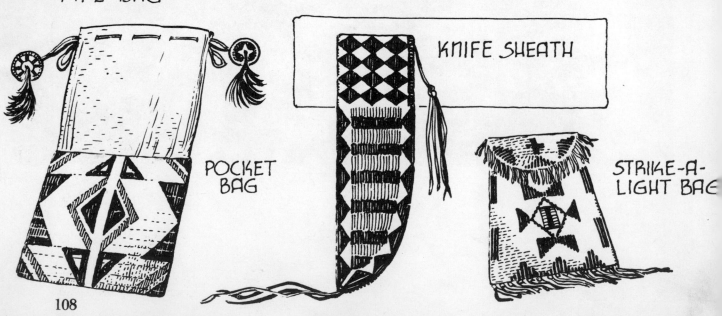

BAGS AND POUCHES—PLAINS

BAGS WERE NEXT in importance to clothing in the everyday life of the Redman—they were his pockets, his tobacco pouch, his pocketbook, his handbag. Important, too, were they to the Indian in gala dress, as something beautiful to carry, richly supplementing the finery of his clothing. There were four types:

The *pipe bag*, one of the most beautiful of Indian items, much coveted by collectors, was made of soft leather and heavily beaded and fringed. It contained the precious ceremonial pipe of its owner. The bag proper consists of a square or rectangular section solidly beaded on both sides, about six inches wide and six to ten inches long. Above this is an extension of about the same size, beaded only with a band or two so that it can be drawn together for tying. At the bottom is a long fringe, sometimes as long as the bag itself, thus often giving the bag an overall length of three feet; the one illustrated measures twenty-six inches.

Pocket bags, sometimes called paint bags, were worn on the belt to serve as a pocket for carrying tobacco, paint, or small trinklets, or in the case of women, sewing materials. They are about six inches wide and lack the long fringe.

Strike-a-light bags carried flint for making fire, and in later years served as a pocketbook. In size they run three by four, or four by five inches.

Knife sheaths of leather were beaded; of rawhide, were painted parfleche-style.

PIPE BAG

POCKET BAG

KNIFE SHEATH

STRIKE-A-LIGHT BAG

BAGS AND POUCHES—WOODLAND

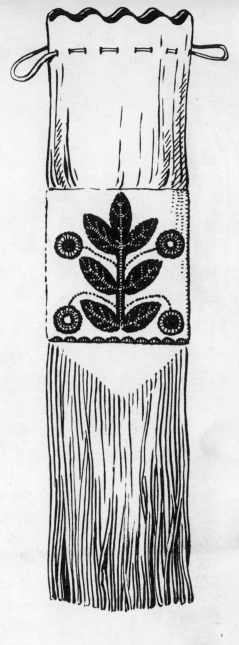

IN SIZE THEY ARE the same as those of the Plains to the westward, and were made in essentially the same way, and served the same functions, but in appearance and atmosphere they were quite different. As the designs of the Woodland tribes differed from those of the prairie peoples, so the beaded bags differed in ornamentation and effect. The one is floral, the other geometric. There is likewise the usual difference in beading technique, the Woodland with the overlaid and the Plains with the lazy stitch.

The *pipe bag* in the illustration is an old Chippewa bag, of the same size as its prairie counterpart on the opposite page, but with the curved floral treatment in contrast to the straight lines of triangles and rectangles. It, too, is the container of its owner's ceremonial pipe and thus becomes an article of importance.

The *pocket bag* below it is but partially beaded, the buckskin itself serving as the background, a treatment equally as prevalent as solid beading. A common practice is to make these bags of *velvet*, to match the dance clothing of the same material.

The little buckskin bag at the left is the Woodland counterpart of the strike-a-light pouch. The knife sheaths were usually solidly beaded as shown.

The most famous of Woodland beaded articles is the huge *medicine bag,* seen in the photograph on page 105. This bag, an old Chippewa one owned by the author, is 18 inches square, with a shoulder strap 8 inches wide and 50 inches long.

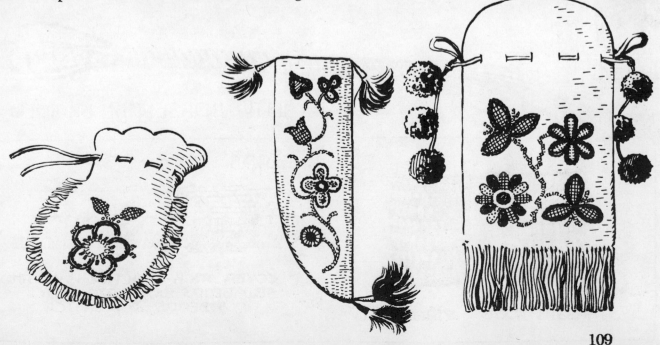

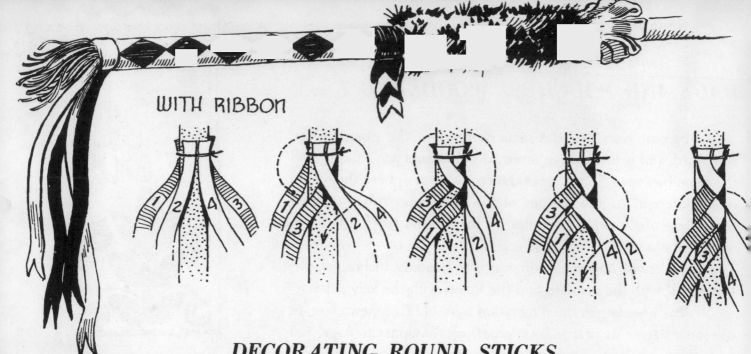

WITH RIBBON

DECORATING ROUND STICKS

ROUND STICKS SUCH AS fancy drumsticks, are often decorated with ribbons of two colors applied by the four-plait method. With the colors placed as in the drawing, the diamond design as shown results, but when both ribbons on one side are of the same color, a spiraled design is produced. Colored yarn tightly wrapped around the stick is also much used. Horsehair, being more substantial, is preferred on articles receiving rough treatment, such as quirts and tomahawk handles. Braid the hair into long strands and wrap around the stick, alternating colors; the projecting strands and loops in the drawing are laid on the stick first and held by the wrapping. Beading, also substantial, requires that the stick be covered with buckskin. Use the lazy stitch (page 105). The beads are usually staggered.

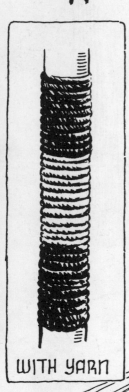

WITH YARN

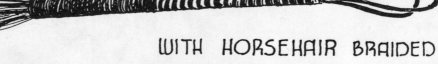

WITH HORSEHAIR BRAIDED

WITH BEADS

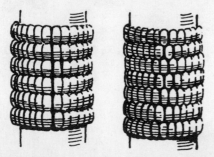

STRAIGHT ROWS   STAGGERED

COVER STICK WITH BUCKSKIN AND SEW BEADS WITH LAZY STITCH — 5 BEADS TO A STITCH

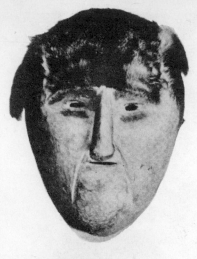

THE APPEAL OF THE solid face is world-wide and timeless. It conjures up the same weird spell, stimulates the same uproarious comedy, among all men. The Indian's use of it is altogether fascinating, both as a craft and as a dance motif.

The mask-makers of greatest fame among the Indians were of two widely separated groups, the Iroquois of the eastern Woodlands, with their Solid-face Society, and the tribes of the Northwest Coast. And their treatment of the art was as far removed from each other as the miles that separate them.

As contrasted to the totem-like masks of the Northwest, remotely and symbolically suggesting animal, bird, and human heads, the solid faces of the Iroquois are realistic and natural, truly human solid faces. This human-like quality is clearly evident in the masks on these pages, all in the possession of the author and obtained from the Cherokees of the Great Smoky Mountain region, a member of the Iroquois family. Fierce, pleasant, witless, or imbecilic, they are nevertheless lifelike, suggesting human types. It is this very human quality that gives these masks their unmatched appeal in dances, for each creates a character of its own, the mask becoming a person whose dancing antics, with facial expression never changing, is unfailing comedy. Even the animal types are realistic rather than totemic.

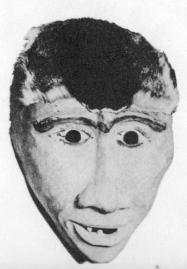

The wood invariably used by the Cherokees is *buckeye;* basswood, white cedar, and pine are also usable. The masks are of such size as to slip easily over the face, extending back to the ears, with ample space in all directions to prevent unpleasant pressure. The average size illustrated is 8½ inches wide, 11 inches high, and 6 to 7 inches deep; the giant mask is 11 by 15 inches.

Cut the block to size, making the backside flat. Shape the face by starting at the forehead and working to the chin—it is largely a matter of jackknife whittling. When roughly shaped, hollow it out to a thickness of ¼ inch, except at the chin which is left ½ inch for strength. Make both eye and nose openings. Color the face reddish-brown and line with black. Attach elastic tape crosswise across the back, and join this to the top of the head with a second elastic. Cover the back with black cloth equipped with tapes to tie around the neck.

Too careful a job in whittling and painting detracts. Bold lines rather than delicate features are needed for carrying power. Try to put character into the face, but guard against overdoing the bizarre effect, remembering that the mask must be true to the Indian type and is not made for use in a Hallowe'en parade.

The dances for these masks I have described in *Dances and Stories of the American Indian.*

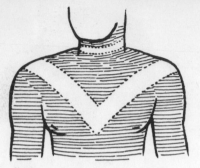

BLUE BODY with YELLOW

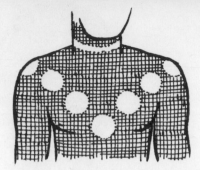

GREEN BODY with FLESH

GRAY BODY with ORANGE

BODY PAINT AND TIGHTS

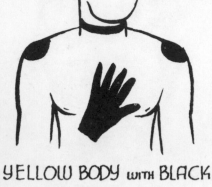

YELLOW BODY with BLACK

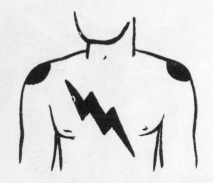

WHITE BODY with BLACK

CARMINE BODY with WHITE

A GLANCE AT THE faces of the dancers in the photographs in these pages will reveal an absence of the "war paint" with which those who affect an Indian make-up usually daub themselves. The Indians did paint their faces, for war and other occasions, not only for the sake of appearance but as a means to magic, to increase their power, both the colors and the designs having symbolic meanings. But their use of it was not as excessive and as gaudy as popularly supposed. The use of war-paint in make-up is dangerous unless very skillfully done, and even then it seldom adds and usually detracts. It is better to leave it alone altogether. The goal is an attractive natural Indian face, best achieved by omitting all such extremes and proceeding as in other types of make-up, using a commercial theatrical paint in reddish-brown Indian color, and shading and lining the eyes as usual.

It is on the *body* and not the face that vivid color and striking design is achieved. In the manner of the Pueblos the body may be painted from head to foot in brilliant and pleasing color. The best showmanship is to set off the leading performers from the rest with special colors, throwing the rank-and-file into the background with bodies of the usual Indian reddish-brown, and painting the leads each in a vivid color of his own. But here again the goal is beauty and not gaudiness or mere showy color.

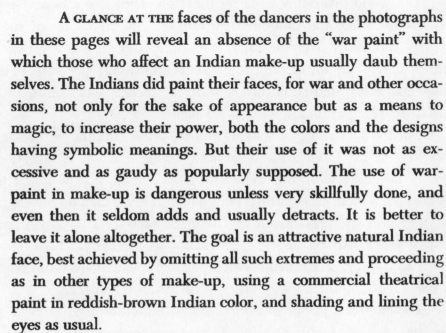

ORANGE BODY
with GRAY

The following body shades have been found effective: ultramarine blue in light shade, canary yellow, soft light green, carmine, gray, and white.

The only make-up suitable for such all-over use is a washable one, removable with soap and water. Grease paint is quite out of the question. Washable make-ups are made with a glycerine base. *Not all paints and pigments are safe to apply to the skin, especially all over—use only standard theatrical preparations.*

The second means of ornamenting the body is *chest designs* and other minor highlights, applied in a contrasting color. Chest designs were widely used on the Plains and in the Southwest. The drawings suggest appropriate patterns; animal outlines, turtles, etc., are also used. Spots at the shoulders point up the shoulders and give them width. Spots above the knee are effective in relieving monotony. Stripes around the upper arm are recommended only when arm bustles are not used. The reddish-brown of the face should be separated from the body color by a half-inch stripe of black around the neck. Likewise the hands, which should match the face color, should be separated.

Combinations of colors are sometimes used, painting half of the body one color and the other half another, or the forearms and lower legs of a different color than the rest, as shown in the sketches. These are extreme efforts for effect and should be used cautiously if at all. It is usually better to rely on the pleasing effect of beautiful all-over color, highlighted with minor contrasts.

When it is not practical to paint the entire body, *tights* become the next choice. While there is no substitute for the flowing muscles of the dancing body, the Indians who dance often frequently find tights a necessity. For this they use ordinary long underwear dyed to the desired color, an example of which is seen on the dancer on the next page. The chest decorations are sewed on. It should be tight-fitting so that it stretches to the exact form. Remove the buttons and substitute hooks and eyes spaced close together.

115

WIGS

HAIR STYLES DIFFER widely but the long-haired wig in the sketch is acceptable for both Plains and midwestern Woodlands.

The photographs in this book reveal a preference for a bobbed wig of less than shoulder length for dancers. These are smart and youthful, unfailing in Indian atmosphere, and are clean in that they do not drag in the body paint.

Wigs may be purchased from theatrical outfitters but good ones are expensive. For a temporary bobbed wig, the cheapest source is to buy a blond "dutch boy" wig of hemp, costing but a few cents, dye it and clip off the bang.

Unexcelled as a substitute for a wig is the black skull-cap seen on the dancer in the photograph, made from a felt hat. These are effective at a distance and are preferable to a poorly made and straggly wig. The type with the ear-covering is recommended.

To make a wig, use black horsehair, binder twine, or hemp rope. If of rope, cut in lengths of 3½ feet, unravel and dye black. Make a tight-fitting muslin skull-cap as shown, and mark a line from front to back to represent the part. Beginning at the front, sew the hair along this line, laying the strands across and attaching them at their middle. Make one or two rows of stitches on the sides as need be to cover the skull-cap, and braid the tassels. Bobbed wigs are first made long and then trimmed on the head.

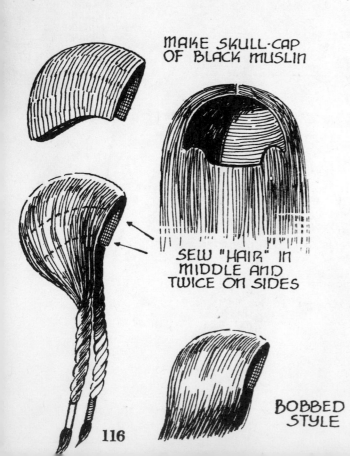

MAKE SKULL-CAP OF BLACK MUSLIN

SEW "HAIR" IN MIDDLE AND TWICE ON SIDES

BOBBED STYLE

116

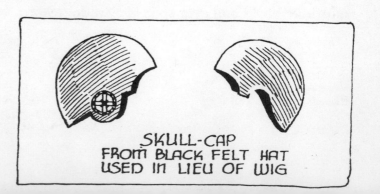

SKULL-CAP FROM BLACK FELT HAT USED IN LIEU OF WIG

INDEX

Angora, 46
Anklets, 46
Antennae, Wire, 9
Aprons, 53
Arm-bands, 50

Bags, Leather, 108, 109
   Parfleche, 90
   Pipe, 108, 109
   Pocket, 108, 109
   Strike-a-light, 108, 109
Baskets, Birchbark, 91
Beading, Lazy stitch, 56, 106
   Loom, 102
   Overlaid stitch, 104
   Plains, 106
   on round sticks, 110
   Woodland, 64, 104
Beads, Bone, 5, 7, 66, 68
   Glass, 102
Beaver fur, 9, 11, 19, 65, 94, 100
Bell protectors, 71
Bells, Dance, 70, 71
Birchbark baskets, 91
   fans, 88
   rattles, 72
Blackfoot, 4, 100
Breastplates, Hair-pipe, 57
   Otter, 58
   Quill, 58
Breechcloths, Dancers', 51
   Plains, 52
   Woodland, 53
Browband—see Headband
Buckskin, Making, 78
   shirts, 55
Buffalo horns, 10
Bullroarers, 74
Bull's tail, 19, 75
Burnt etching, 99
Bustle, Butterfly, 40
   Crow, 43, 44
   Feather, 30
   Hair, 28
   Oklahoma, 37
   Sioux, 32
   styles, 44, 45
   Sunburst, 42
   tricks, 34
   U-shaped, 41
Butterfly bustle, 40
Buttons, 40

Calumets, 93

Cartridge-shell necklace, 68
Catlinite, 96
Cherokee, 73, 112
Chippewa, 8, 9, 11, 12, 13, 18, 21, 47, 48,
   50, 53, 61, 80, 82, 83, 87, 88, 93, 98,
   100, 104, 109, 112
Chippewa feather crest, 8
Concha, 66
Coup feathers, 3
Coup-sticks, 87
Crow bustle, 43, 44
Cuffs, Plains, 56
   Woodland, 60

Designs, Floral, 48, 53, 55, 104, 109
   Geometric, 48, 53, 56, 106, 109
   Parfleche, 90
   Rosette, 17
   Shield, 86
Dewclaws, 68, 69, 70
Dog-soldiers, 87
Dresses, Plains, 62, 63
   Woodland, 64, 65
Drums, Hoop, 80
   Log, 82
   Tub, 82
   Water, 82
Drumsticks, 83

Ear hangings, 66
Elk's teeth, 66
Ermine tails, 7
Etching, Burnt, 99

Fans, 88
Feather crest, 8
Feather roach, 26, 27
Feathers, Ornamental, 89
   Roach, 24, 25
   Top, 24, 25
   To straighten, 34
   War-bonnet, 3
Fire coloration, 98
Floral design, 48, 55, 104, 109
Fluffie fringe, 69
Fur tassels, 100

Geometric design, 48, 56, 106, 109
Graining tool, 77

Hair bustles, 28
Hair feathers, 19
Hair-pipes, 57
Hair roach, 20

Hat, Woodland, 11, 23
   Woman's, 65
Headband, Beaded, 12, 13, 19
   Leather, 16
   War-bonnet, 5
   with rosette, 14
Headdress
   Feather crest, 8
   Feather roach, 26, 27
   Hair feathers, 19
   Headbands, 12, 13
   Horn, 10
   Turbans, 18, 19
   Wapeginicki, 19
   War-bonnet, 2
   Woman's, 65
   Woodland hat, 11
Hoofs—see Dewclaws
Hopi, 55, 74
Horn headdress, 10
Horsehair, 3, 21, 28, 110

Iroquois, 112

Karak, 89
Knife sheaths, 108, 109

Leg-bands, 47
Leggings, Plains, 52
   Women's, 62
   Woodland, 53
List cloth, 52
Loom, Beading, 102

Major plume, 6
Make-up, 114
Makuks, 91
Masks, 112
Moccasins, 48, 49
Moraches, 74

Necklaces, 66, 67, 68

Otters, 58

Paint, Body, 114
Parfleche, 90
Peace pipe, 95
Pipe bags, 108, 109
Pipe bowls, 96
Pipestems, 93, 94, 95
Pipestone, 96
Pipe-tomahawk, 95
Plaiting, 110
Pogamogans, 75
Pompons, 50, 101
Porcupine hair, 21
   quills, 58
Pueblo, 114

Quill-work, 58
Quiver, 91

Rattles, Birchbark, 72
   Dewclaw, 68, 69, 70
   Gourd, 72
   Horn, 72
   Rawhide, 72
   Tin-can, 72
   Tin-jingle, 69, 72
   Turtle, 73
Rawhide, 76, 77, 90
Roach, Feather, 26, 27
   Hair, 20
Roach feathers, 24, 25
Rosette, Arm, 28
   designs, 17
   Embroidery floss, 16
   Feather, 14, 15, 16
   Forehead, 14, 15, 16
   Hair, 12, 28

Shields, 85
Shirts, Buckskin, 55
   Hopi, 55
   Plains, 54
   Woodland, 55
Sioux, 2, 4, 32, 48, 50, 52, 53, 59
Skull-cap, 21, 116
Skunk fur, 11, 19
Sleighbells, 70, 71
Solid faces, 112
Spears, 87
Steatite, 96
Sunbursts, 42

Tassels, Fur, 100
   Hair, 54
   Yarn, 101
Thimbles, 64, 69
Tights, 115
Tin jingles, 64, 69, 72, 73
Tomahawk, 95
Tomtoms—see Drums
Turbans, 18, 19
Turtles, 73

U-Shaped bustles, 41

Vests, Plains, 56
   Woodland, 60

War-bonnet, 4
War clubs, 75
War paint, 114
Wigs, 116
Wapeginicki, 19
Woodland hat, 11, 23

Yarn leg-bands, 47
   tassels, 101
   wrapping, 110

118